Not Reformed at All

Books by John W. Robbins

Answer to Ayn Rand, 1974

The Case Against Indexation, 1976

The Case for Gold (author and editor), 1982

God's Hammer: The Bible and Its Critics (editor), 1982, 1987, 1995

Scripture Twisting in the Seminaries: Feminism, 1985

Cornelius Van Til: The Man and the Myth, 1986

Education, Christianity and the State (editor), 1987, 2004

Pat Robertson: A Warning to America, 1988

Gordon H. Clark: Personal Recollections
(author and editor), 1989

Essays on Ethics and Politics (editor), 1992

A Man of Principle: Essays in Honor of Hans F. Sennholz
(author and editor), 1992

Against the World: The Trinity Review 1978-1988
(author and editor), 1996

Without a Prayer: Ayn Rand and the Close of Her System, 1997

Ancient Philosophy (editor), 1997

Ecclesiastical Megalomania: The Economic and Political Thought of the Roman Catholic Church, 1999

The Church Effeminate (author and editor), 2001

Against the Churches: The Trinity Review 1989-1998
(author and editor), 2002

Christ and Civilization, 2003

A Companion to The Current Justification Controversy
(author and editor), 2003

Not Reformed at All: Medievalism in "Reformed" Churches
(co-author), 2004

Not Reformed at All

Medievalism in "Reformed" Churches

John Robbins and Sean Gerety

The Trinity Foundation

Cover: Pieter Brueghel the Younger (1564-1636). *The Parable of the Blindmen.* Oil on wood, 122 x 170 cm. RF 829. Photo: Hervé Lewandowski. Photo credit: Réunion des Musées Nationaux/Art Resource, New York. Louvre, Paris, France.

Not Reformed at All
Medievalism in "Reformed" Churches

Published by
The Trinity Foundation
Post Office Box 68
Unicoi, Tennessee 37692
http://www.trinityfoundation.org/
ISBN: 0-940931-66-4

Contents

Foreword

In 2002 Douglas Wilson published a book titled *"Reformed" Is Not Enough: Recovering the Objectivity of the Covenant.* Had the book presented merely his own opinions, it would have required some comment, for Wilson is widely known as a leader in the so-called Classical-Christian school movement; but the book represents more than Wilson's own opinions: It is a manifesto for another movement in which Wilson is a major figure, which has variously been called Neolegalism, Hypercovenantalism, Shepherdism, the Moscow-Monroe Axis, Federal Vision, and Auburn Avenue Theology. This movement is led by men who, like Wilson, occupy positions of influence and income in nominally Reformed churches: James Jordan, Steve Wilkins, Peter Leithart, Mark Horne, John Armstrong, Steve Schlissel, John Barach, Norman Shepherd, and Andrew Sandlin, to name a few.

There have been a few disciplinary actions taken against this movement in some Presbyterian church courts, but those actions have been largely ineffective. Only when Christians in the pews understand the doctrinal issues will there be any effective action taken against these heretical doctrines and the men who teach them, for most pastors are either too uninformed, too undiscerning, too timid, or too chummy with these men to honor and obey their vows to preserve, protect, and defend the Gospel; and too callous and unloving to protect the souls they have sworn to protect from false teaching.

The treason of the "Reformed" clergy is widespread, and it takes two forms: the actual propagation of heresy, and the defense of heresy from criticism and discipline. For every pastor who commits the first kind of treason, there are ten who commit the second. This book is intended to inform ordinary Christians, who elect and pay the salaries of the clergy, about the treason of the"Reformed" clergy, so that they will be able to take appropriate action to end it.

1. The Revolution Was

Some just waking from their theological slumbers have heard that there is a Revolution in progress in American Presbyterian churches. But the Revolution is nearly over.

The Revolution started 60 years ago, and it has virtually defeated conservative American Presbyterianism. The Liberal leavening of American churches began in the nineteenth century and eventually led to the formation of conservative bodies in the early twentieth century. Those conservative bodies themselves were corrupted by movements of thought that almost no one recognized as alien to Scripture. Few realized what was afoot, and those who did, and spoke out, were ignored, ridiculed, or attacked.

One of the few who both understood the Revolution and opposed it was Dr. Gordon H. Clark. Over the course of his career as a Christian philosopher and theologian,[1] he published about 40 books based on the rather simple ideas that God has spoken to men in Scripture; he has spoken in human language so that men might understand; and the words he has

1. Dr. Clark taught at the University of Pennsylvania, Wheaton College, Reformed Episcopal Seminary, Butler University (where he was Chairman of the Department of Philosophy for 28 years), Covenant College, and Sangre de Cristo Seminary. He was an Elder (both teaching and ruling, if one can distinguish the two) in six Presbyterian denominations (leaving each one behind as it left the Word of God behind), and wrote 40 books, including the best history of philosophy in the English language, *Thales to Dewey*.

spoken are divine truth. These simple ideas were denied, not simply by recognized theological Liberals, but by many who professed to be Bible-believing Conservatives. Their attack on these ideas was the first wave of the Revolution. It came as a surprise attack, an ambush, of Dr. Clark by the faculty of Westminster Theological Seminary in Philadelphia in 1944.

The faculty of the Seminary, including Professors Cornelius Van Til, John Murray, R. B. Kuiper, and Ned Stonehouse, sought to depose Dr. Clark without trial from the ministry of the Orthodox Presbyterian Church (OPC). Their procedural ploy was to say that Dr. Clark's examination for and ordination to the office of minister were too hastily conducted. But the main thrust of their attack was an attempt to discredit Dr. Clark's theology and philosophy without being required to prove in court that his theology was in error. Dr. Clark successfully repelled the sinful (and unrepented) attack of the Westminster Seminary faculty, and he remained in the Orthodox Presbyterian ministry. But when the Westminster faculty launched a similar attack on one of Dr. Clark's defenders, immediately after being defeated in their reprehensible attempt to defrock Dr. Clark, the supporters of Dr. Clark (one-third of the fledgling denomination, including its largest congregation) left the Orthodox Presbyterian Church in disgust, and Dr. Clark reluctantly went with them. Rather than resist the Seminary faculty for another three years on essentially the same issues, a faculty that had already shown itself to value neither the peace nor the purity of the church, they left. Their leaving may have been a serious mistake, for it left the errorists without significant opposition in both the Seminary and the denomination, and they were free to teach their un-Biblical opinions to generations of students. As a result, the irrational theology of the Dark Ages, channeled principally through Professors Herman Bavinck and Cornelius Van Til, and embellished by the doctrinal oddities of John Murray,[2] became the dominant view in the churches served by Westminster Seminary. This was the theological matrix of much error to come.[3] The first wave of the Revolution was successful. Though they had lost the battle to depose Dr. Clark, the Revolutionaries remained in control of both Westminster Seminary and the Orthodox Presbyterian Church.

In 1957, Dr. Clark revisited the battle for intelligible, propositional revelation that had occurred in the 1940s, summarized the views of both sides, and articulated once again several of the arguments he had made in the debates of that decade. One of those arguments concerned the theological agnosticism of the faculty of Westminster Seminary, who taught that man, because of his creatureliness, finitude, and sinfulness, could have only an analogy of divine truth, not divine truth itself. In their own words, "We dare not maintain that his [God's] knowledge and our [men's] knowledge coincide at any single point." They repudiated another view of knowledge because that view implied that "a proposition would have to have the same meaning for God as for man," which they said was impossible.

To which Dr. Clark replied:

> If God has the truth, and if man has only an analogy, it follows that he [man] does not have the truth. An analogy of the truth is not the truth.... If the human mind were limited to analogical truths, it could never know the univocal truth that it was limited to analogies.... This theory, therefore, whether found in [the Roman Catho-

2. Even such a stalwart disciple of Van Til as Mark Karlberg admits that Murray set the stage for the emergence and triumph of Neolegalism at Westminster Seminary in the 1970s. See Mark Karlberg, *The Changing of the Guard*, The Trinity Foundation, 2001.

3. See "The Heresy Matrix," *The Trinity Review*, September/October 2003; available in the Review Archives at www.trinityfoundation.org.

> lic] Thomas Aquinas, [the Neo-orthodox] Emil Brunner, or professed conservatives, is unrelieved skepticism and is incompatible with the acceptance of a divine revelation of the truth.... Such skepticism must be completely repudiated if we wish to safeguard a doctrine of verbal revelation.[4]

Dr. Clark might have added, "if we wish to safeguard any doctrine of Scripture whatsoever, since they all depend on verbal revelation."

During subsequent decades there were skirmishes and battles in the theological Revolution as those who denied that men could understand divine truth made forays into other doctrinal areas. From 1975 to 1982 a controversy over the views of Norman Shepherd, a member of the Westminster Seminary Faculty since 1963, occupied the attention of the Philadelphia Presbytery in the Orthodox Presbyterian Church and the Westminster Seminary faculty and administration. The faculty and administration were now defending one of their own – a teacher approved by the Old Guard to succeed Professor John Murray in the Systematics Department, a teacher defended by Professor Cornelius Van Til, Professor Richard B. Gaffin, Jr., Professor John Frame, and by a majority of the faculty members at Westminster Seminary – against charges that he was teaching the heresy of justification by faith and works.[5] Paralyzed by the paradoxical theology of Van Til, both Westminster Seminary and the Orthodox Presbyterian Church failed to preserve, protect, and defend the Gospel against the heresy of covenantal Neolegalism in the Shepherd controversy. Professor Shepherd left both Westminster Seminary and the

4. "The Bible As Truth," in *God's Hammer: The Bible and Its Critics*. The Trinity Foundation, 1982, 33-34.

5. For a detailed account of this controversy, see O. Palmer Robertson, *The Current Justification Controversy*. The Trinity Foundation, 2003.

Orthodox Presbyterian Church in good standing and joined the Christian Reformed Church, where he subsequently pastored congregations for almost two decades. Although he had been removed from the faculty, his teaching continued at Westminster Seminary.[6]

Norman Shepherd is but the tip of the Neolegalist iceberg floating in the Reformed sea. Because there was no disciplinary judgment against Shepherd by any ecclesiastical body, and because the ground had been prepared for his confusion concerning covenant and justification by the Vantilian confusion about God and revelation, Shepherd's teaching attracted more and more followers. Once again a few recognized the error and spoke out. In the summer of 1999, Illiana Presbytery in the Presbyterian Church in America tried and deposed a man from the ministry for sacerdotalism. He was a protégé of Reconstructionist writer James Jordan, a student and supporter of Norman Shepherd. Despite being deposed from the ministry in the PCA, Burke Shade was recognized and accepted as a minister in good standing by Douglas Wilson's new denomination, the Confederation of Reformed Evangelicals.

In June 2002 another pocket of resistance to the Revolution appeared: Covenant Presbytery of the Reformed Presbyterian Church in the United States (RPCUS) denounced a number of old heresies in new frocks and issued a "Call to Repentance" to the speakers at the 2002 Auburn Avenue Presbyterian Church Pastors Conference sponsored by the Presbyterian Church in America (PCA) congregation in Monroe, Louisiana. One of the errors the RPCUS denounced was belittling revealed propositional truth. The list of those charged and urged to repent included PCA Pastor Steven Wilkins of the Auburn

6. See Mark Karlberg, *The Changing of the Guard*; and O. Palmer Robertson, *The Current Justification Controversy*.

Avenue Presbyterian Church; Pastor Steven Schlissel of Messiah's Congregation in Brooklyn, New York; United Reformed Church of North America Pastor John Barach; and Douglas Wilson, Pastor of Christ Church in Moscow, Idaho, and leader of an ecclesiastical-educational complex that includes *Credenda-Agenda* magazine, New St. Andrews College, The Logos School, Canon Press, and the Confederation of Reformed Evangelicals. Norman Shepherd had been scheduled to speak at the 2002 Auburn Avenue Pastors Conference, but due to the death of his wife, he was unable to attend. So, while Shepherd's name was not included in the list of those charged by the RPCUS with attempting to destroy the Reformed Faith, his Scripturally-aberrant views have been examined in recent issues of *The Trinity Review.*[7]

In 2003 one church in the Orthodox Presbyterian Church (OPC) convicted an Elder, John Kinnaird, a disciple and defender of Norman Shepherd, of teaching justification by faith and works, contrary to the Scriptures and the *Westminster Confession*, and that Session's decision, when appealed to the Philadelphia Presbytery of the OPC, was initially upheld. But Kinnaird's conviction was subsequently overturned by the General Assembly of the Orthodox Presbyterian Church in June 2003, which found his teaching to be compatible with the *Westminster Confession* and the Scriptures. The Revolution was triumphant. The epistemological heresy of the 1940s had blossomed into the soteriological heresy of the third millennium. Dark Age philosophy had given birth to Dark Age theology.

7. See the September and October 2001 issues – "False Shepherd"; and the March and April 2001 issues – "The Changing of the Guard." All are available in the Review Archives at www.trinityfoundation.org. Shepherd subsequently spoke at the Auburn Avenue Presbyterian Church in October 2003.

2. Theological Sophistry

In late 2002, Douglas Wilson wrote a book setting forth his theological opinions. *"Reformed" Is Not Enough* is a manifesto, a book-length defense of the Revolution. It is a response, in part, to the public rebuke the RPCUS issued to Wilson and his friends in June 2002. And it is a contumacious defense: Wilson's book contains no apology for creating misunderstanding or confusion; it admits no error, not even in choice of words; it shows no sign of contrition, repentance, or reconciliation. It is a stubborn defense of his views. Far from clarifying or correcting matters, Wilson exacerbated the situation by truculently defending and compounding his error.

Wilson defends his views by using these rhetorical devices and debate tricks:

1. Wilson quotes incomplete passages of Scripture, even breaking off in mid-sentence, that mislead the reader.

2. Wilson makes assertions, and offers no Scripture to support his assertions.

3. Wilson misinterprets Scripture.

4. Wilson ignores and omits Scriptural statements that disprove his contentions.

5. Wilson rejects the logical system of truth in the *Westminster Confession*, while claiming to defend the "historic Reformed" position.

6. Wilson redefines crucial terms.

7. Wilson makes misleading analogies and illustrations.

8. Wilson constructs invalid arguments.

9. Wilson is incoherent, accepting on one page what he rejects on another.

10. Wilson presents caricatures of opposing arguments, and then ridicules the caricatures, misleading readers into thinking he has refuted the arguments.

11. Wilson presents what he calls the "historic Reformed" position by quoting moderns almost exclusively.

12. Wilson offers no argument for the central thesis of his book, that "historic Reformed views" have been misunderstood because modern Presbyterians have been influenced by the so-called Rationalism of the Enlightenment.

13. Wilson accuses falsely.

We will give examples from his book of each of these practices.

3. The Matrix

Wilson's book is not original, but entirely derivative, and his comments, footnotes, and bibliography make it clear from whom he derives his ideas. His footnotes belie his claim to be defending "historic Reformed" theology: Virtually all of them (75 of 78) are citations of twentieth and twenty-first century writers, including Internet theologians. There are only two footnotes in Wilson's book to "pre-Enlightenment" writers: John Calvin and John Newton (and we're generously giving Wilson Newton, since Newton lived in the eighteenth century, the century of the Enlightenment). Wilson's bibliography is just as lopsided: Only two entries – again Newton and Calvin – are "pre-Enlightenment." The rest – 27 – are all moderns: Lewis Schenck, Joel Garver, Randy Booth, John Frame, Peter Leithart, Rich Lusk, Keith Mathison, etc. Not only are they moderns, but nearly all of them have adopted views similar to those of Norman Shepherd on justification, covenant, election, and the sacraments. Shepherd (and James Jordan) are the unacknowledged sources of Wilson's ideas, and reading *"Reformed" Is Not Enough* is like re-reading Shepherd's essays and lectures.[8] After reviewing his footnotes and bibli-

8. See O. Palmer Robertson, *The Current Justification Controversy*.

ography, one doubts that Wilson has even read the "pre-Enlightenment" men whose views he claims to be defending.

Wilson's principal contribution to the debate surrounding covenantal Neolegalism is a facile glibness and an adolescent smart-aleckness that readers of his magazine and books apparently find attractive. As one observer put it, Wilson's attitude seems to be:

> My name is Doug,
> I am so cool:
> 'Til you agree,
> You are a fool.

Wilson informs us that he is "postmillennial, Calvinistic, presbyterian, Van Tillian, theonomic, and reformed" (8). He refers to his "Reformed and medieval mindset" (9).[9] Given that mélange of ideas, one can understand why his book is so confused. But the book, like many irrational documents and persons, betrays an underlying consistency – one just has to read closely to see it. Van Til's philosophy is agnostic and his theology irrational, and they are the context in which Wilson writes. Two of Wilson's bêtes noires are what he calls "rationalism," which he fails to define, and "ethereal," "invisible" things that cannot be photographed. The European medievals, before whom Wilson genuflects, were as sensate and superstitious as any people who have lived on the planet.[10]

4. Dodging the Charge of Heresy

One way to try to escape the charge of heresy is to redefine the word *heresy* by placing it in some truncated and obsolete

9. Wilson spells "Reformed" both with an initial capital and without; there seems to be no rhyme or reason for the variation.

10. See John Robbins, *Christ and Civilization.* The Trinity Foundation, 2003.

context. This is the method of escape that Andrew Sandlin tries to use to defend himself as well as others. He argues that while the Christian faith *may* be best expressed in the statements of the *Westminster Confession* and the Reformed creeds, heresy is determined "primarily" by deviations from the so-called "ecumenical" or "classical" creeds. In his defense of the speakers at the Auburn Avenue Pastors Conference Sandlin argued:

> I start from historic, orthodox Christianity anchored in the ecumenical Christian creeds – what Thomas Oden would call "classical Christianity." I see the Reformed Faith as the capstone, not the foundation, of Christian orthodoxy. It's the finish line, not the starting gate.... [H]eresy is almost always defined in terms of deviation from classical Christianity, not from the distinctives of any particular species of the (orthodox) church, even the Presbyterian Church. So, even if the men [Wilson, Wilkins, Schlissel, Barach] charged [by the RPCUS] are not Reformed (and I believe they are; they claim to be), they are not thereby heretics....[11]

By this low standard, one could argue that the 1992/1994 *Catholic Catechism* is within the bounds of orthodoxy.

In Sandlin's view, the Reformed faith, far from being necessary, is simply the shingles on the roof. The foundation is the "ecumenical creeds." The building is "classical Christianity." Notice that Sandlin's faith is not anchored in the Scriptures, but in the "ecumenical creeds" – that is, uninspired documents accepted by several branches of "Christendom." The Reformed Faith, while not exactly superfluous, is neither foundational nor structural. According to Sandlin's scheme, a man is not a

11. It should be pointed out that Sandlin was supported in his defense of these men and his attack on Joe Morecraft of the RPCUS by Gary North, who has since criticized Sandlin for relying too heavily on Oscar Cullman.

heretic if he denies, say, justification by faith alone, since it is a doctrine peculiar to the Reformed Faith, a doctrine that is not accepted by either Orthodoxism or Romanism, and which is not mentioned in any "ecumenical creed." Nor, according to Sandlin's scheme, is a man a heretic if he denies the sufficiency and inerrancy of Scripture, since those doctrines are not mentioned in the "ecumenical creeds" and are in fact denied by the Romanists and the Orthodoxists.[12] Nor is a man a heretic if he advocates the use of images and statues in worship, since both the Orthodoxists and the Romanists use and advocate the use of such "aids to worship," and the "ecumenical creeds" do not condemn their use. One could go on at length, but by now the reader should get the point: Sandlin has rejected Biblical Christianity in favor of something he calls "classical Christianity."[13]

Wilson, while I'm sure he appreciates Sandlin's jumping to his defense, as well as Sandlin's "classical Christianity" subterfuge, apparently doesn't want to hide behind the vagueness of some ancient creeds. Wilson wants to do two things: (1) to wrap himself in the Reformed confessions, particularly the *Westminster Confession*; and (2) paradoxically claim that "Reformed is not enough." Rather than truncating the Christian faith as Sandlin does in good fundamentalist fashion, Wilson wants to augment and correct it by adding fresh, new insights. But upon examination, his corrections and insights turn out to be errors rejected by the Reformers and defended by several varieties of heretical theologians. Wilson, like Sandlin, also repudiates Biblical Christianity, but he is not so candid about it. Wilson writes:

12. Not to be confused with orthodontists, who actually do some people good.

13. See John Robbins, "The Gospel of Jesus Christ Versus Neolegalism." *The Trinity Review*, August/September 2002. The essay can be found in the Review Archives at www.trinityfoundation.org. F. J. DeAngelis has collected some Sandlin quotations demonstrating his abandonment of Reformed theology at http://www.semper-reformanda.org/sandlin.html.

> It is our conviction that certain epistemological developments since the Enlightenment have caused many *modern* conservative Calvinists to read their confessions in a spirit alien to that which produced them. As a result, we [Wilkins, Schlissel, Barach, and Wilson] were taken to task [by the RPCUS] for denying our confessional heritage in just those places where we were in fact upholding it.... Our opponents say the confession is right as it gets – biblical Christianity in "its purest human expression" – and then proceed to merrily disregard what the confession actually teaches in this area [7-8; emphasis in the original].

This paragraph is typical of Wilson's style. Wilson makes an assertion, crucial to his own argument, but he fails to inform his readers what those pernicious "epistemological developments" were, much less to show how they have caused modern Presbyterians to misread the *Westminster Confession.* Like so much else in this book, Wilson simply makes a statement and expects his readers to accept it. His thought and writing are episodic and oracular; he ejaculates ipsedixitisms and expects his readers to accept them. In many cases his expectations are met, which demonstrates the gullibility of many of his readers and their own inability to think rationally. Rather than providing valid arguments from true premises, Wilson offers his "conviction" that this or that is so. His appeal to "conviction" fits his irrational, anti-intellectual philosophy, but it carries no probative weight. Rather, it reveals Wilson's intellectual bankruptcy.

Wilson claims to be upholding the "historic Reformed faith" against the "modern rationalistic" Calvinists. He is double-minded even about this. On the one hand, Wilson claims to be a "pre-Enlightenment medieval" defending the allegedly proper medieval reading of the *Westminster Con-*

fession.[14] On the other hand, he tells us that "we must not be allowed to assume that the last significant attainment [in theology] was in the middle of the seventeenth century [the time of the writing of the *Westminster Confession*]" (13). He apparently thinks he and some other moderns have made "significant attainments" in theology that are superior to the Westminster Standards. Double-mindedness is a recurring pattern in his book.

5. Tradition

Wilson writes: "...over the centuries the Church grows into a deeper and richer understanding of the faith" (49). Now, this ambiguous statement may or may not be true. If Wilson means by the word "Church" a visible organization – and his rejection of the notion of the invisible church seems to make that meaning mandatory for him – then, contrary to what he says, there have been retrograde movements in the organized church's understanding of the faith. First, there was a retrogression in understanding after the apostles died. Despite the efforts of church councils, that retrogression in understanding deepened for more than a thousand years and was not significantly corrected until the sixteenth century, when God poured out his Spirit on Western Europe and the Christian Reformation occurred. Since the writing of the *Westminster Confession of Faith* in the seventeenth century, the organized churches have again declined in their understanding of the Christian faith, abandoning the Reformation creeds and confessions, to the point that most of those organizations that call

14. Wilson's chronology seems to be slightly askew. The *Westminster Confession* was written in the 1640s, hardly the Middle Ages. The Reformation and Renaissance had occurred more than a century earlier. The modern world, Wilson's bête noir, was already well-developed.

themselves churches are apostate at the beginning of the twenty-first century. There has been progress in understanding – the *Westminster Confession* is far superior to any preceding or succeeding creed or confession, as reading Schaff's compilation of creeds and confessions will easily show – but that progress is neither steady nor permanent. There has been retrogression as well; in fact, most of the history of organized churches is a retrograde movement in their understanding of the Christian faith, interrupted by brilliant, short bursts of Spirit-given insight, such as occurred in the first century and again in the sixteenth century, with isolated individuals here and there shining brightly in dark centuries as witnesses to the faithfulness of God to his remnant. The natural tendency of churches is toward apostasy, not spiritual growth. Today we are in a long period of retrogression in ecclesiastical understanding of the faith, thanks in part to attacks on the intellect by the eighteenth-century, German, Enlightenment philosopher Immanuel Kant and his disciples.[15] But Wilson wants us

15. "The anti-intellectual tendency in the modern world is no trifling thing; it has its roots deep in the entire philosophical development of modern times. Modern philosophy since the days of Kant, with the theology that has been influenced by it, has had as its dominant note, certainly as its present day result, a depreciation of the reason and a skeptical answer to Pilate's question, 'What is truth?' This attack upon the intellect has been conducted by men of marked intellectual power; but an attack upon the intellect it has been all the same. And at last the logical results of it, even in the sphere of practice, are beginning to appear. A marked characteristic of the present day is a lamentable intellectual decline, which has appeared in all fields of human endeavor except those that deal with purely material things. The intellect has been browbeaten so long in theory that one cannot be surprised if it is now ceasing to function in practice....

"As over against this anti-intellectual tendency in the modern world, it will be one chief purpose of the present little book to defend the primacy of the intellect, and in particular to break down the false and disastrous opposition which has been set up between knowledge and faith.... As a matter of fact, all true faith involves an intellectual element; all [Christian] faith involves knowledge and issues in knowledge" (J. Gresham Machen, *What Is Faith?* 26, 51).

Note that Machen actually understood Enlightenment and modern philosophy, while Wilson does not. Machen understood that modern philosophy is proto believe that progress in understanding the faith has been pretty steady, even during the Dark Ages. The results of this imaginary progress he calls "tradition."

Wilson distinguishes three views of tradition: "(1) authoritative tradition as *equal* to Scripture; (2) authoritative tradition as *subordinate* to Scripture; and (3) tradition as *absolute*" (50). He asserts that "the first developed during the middle ages.... The second is the position of historical Protestantism.... The third is the position held by individualist sectarians..." (50).[16]

Now, what is wrong with Wilson's taxonomy of tradition? First, it is incomplete. It is as if one were to classify words grammatically, and omit nouns. We suspect there is a good reason for Wilson's omissions: To mention other views of the relationship between tradition and Scripture, or to offer a complete taxonomy, would destroy Wilson's argument. This is an old trick: Offer your readers or listeners alternatives, but omit the correct alternative. This trick has been used very effectively in both politics and theology. In politics, socialism, which is called left-wing, has been touted as the only alternative to fascism, which is called right-wing, and vice versa. At present in America, a faith-based welfare state is offered as the only alternative to a secular welfare state. In theology, legalism is touted as the alternative to antinomianism, and vice versa. In all these cases, the genuine alternative is omitted, and poison is offered as the antidote for poison. That makes the out-

---

foundly irrational and anti-intellectual, due to the influence of one of the major figures of the Enlightenment, Immanuel Kant. But Wilson thinks modern philosophy is "rationalistic" and "intellectual." Wilson, in his anti-intellectualism, is an unwitting disciple of Kant, and even proposes, as we shall see later, vulgar Kantian versions of the church, covenant, election, and justification.

16. Wilson seems to have taken his misleading views on tradition from Keith Mathison, an employee of R. C. Sproul's Ligonier Ministries. Canon Press publishes Mathison's books. Who these "individualist sectarians" are who hold to an "absolute tradition," Wilson, of course, does not say.

come certain: Whichever alternative churchgoers (or voters) choose will be wrong.

Wilson omits – intentionally or out of ignorance, the reader must judge – a fourth view of tradition, which is actually the historic Protestant position. Notice that his three categories all describe tradition as "authoritative" or "absolute." But the historic Protestant view is that tradition has no authority in the church, and tradition is never absolute. That view is stated very clearly in the first chapter of the *Westminster Confession of Faith*, which Wilson claims to defend. By omitting the *Confession's* view from his list, Wilson smuggles in at the beginning of his argument what he is required prove. This fallacy is called begging the question.[17] It allows him to befuddle many of his readers and to persuade some of them that his view really is the historic Protestant view.

Chapter 1 of the *Westminster Confession* says, "the books commonly called Apocrypha, not being of divine inspiration, are no part of the canon of the Scripture; and therefore are of no authority in the Church of God..." (*WCF* 1.3). Notice that because the Apocryphal books are not divinely inspired, they are not Scripture; and because they are not Scripture, *they are of no authority in the church of God*. The historic Protestant position on theological and ecclesiastical authority is Scripture alone, not Scripture plus tradition. The *Confession* summarizes Scripture's own view of Scripture:

> The whole counsel of God, concerning all things necessary for his own glory, man's salvation, faith, and life, is either expressly set down in Scripture, or by good and necessary consequence may be deduced from Scripture,

17. Many use the phrase "beg(ging) the question" incorrectly to mean something such as "This question (whatever the question is) demands an answer." To "beg the question" means to assume a proposition that requires proof.

> unto which nothing at any time is to be added, whether by new revelations of the Spirit or traditions of men [*WCF* 1.6].

Please note the words "whole," "all," "nothing," "any," and "traditions." The authors of the *Confession* implicitly and explicitly ruled out tradition as an authority either in the church considered corporately or for the individual believer:

> The supreme Judge, by which all controversies of religion are to be determined, and all decrees of councils, opinions of ancient writers, doctrines of men, and private spirits, are to be examined, and in whose sentence we are to rest, can be no other but the Holy Spirit speaking in the Scripture [*WCF* 1.10].

Please note the words "all" (used twice), "decrees of councils," "opinions of ancient writers," "no other," and "Scripture." All tradition is subject to the supreme judge, which is Scripture alone. Tradition is not on the bench, but in the dock. Tradition – the decrees of councils and opinions of ancient writers – is under the absolute and authoritative judgment of Scripture. Far from being the standard of judgment or an authority, the decrees of councils and opinions of ancient writers are to be judged by Scripture alone:

> The infallible rule of interpretation of Scripture is the Scripture itself; and therefore, when there is a question about the true and full sense of any Scripture (which is not manifold, but one), it must be searched and known by other places that speak more clearly [*WCF* 1.9].

Please note the words "The" and "must." Scripture is the only infallible rule of interpreting Scripture. Decrees of councils, private spirits, new revelations, and opinions of ancient writers are not infallible rules of interpretation. The true and full sense, which is one sense, not many, "must" be found by comparing Scripture with Scripture.

The historic Protestant position, as represented by the *Westminster Confession of Faith*, which Wilson claims to be upholding, contradicts Wilson: Scripture is the sole authority because it alone is inspired by God. Scripture is self-interpreting and does not need an interpretive authority, such as tradition. Scripture is sufficient, clear, final, and wholly in writing. Scripture is the standard by which all the opinions of all men, ancient and modern, all the decrees of all church councils, and all other traditions are to be judged. Logical deductions from Scripture by "good and necessary consequence" possess the same authority as Scripture itself, for the *Logos* is God, and God is rational and logical and means what he says. God's revelation is not contradictions or analogical truths. Scripture is the actual words of God (see *John* 17),and therefore it is the sole authority. Scripture judges all traditions; it is neither judged by tradition nor dependent on tradition for its proper interpretation. No tradition is to be added to Scripture, whether one calls that tradition authoritative, subordinate, or absolute.

In contrast to the Biblical view summarized by the *Confession*, Wilson explains his view of authoritative tradition: "The second [which Wilson incorrectly claims is the historic Protestant position] says that the traditions of the Church are authoritative, but are not infallible or ultimate" (51). Not only does the *Westminster Confession* deny that tradition is authoritative in its first chapter, but Wilson cites no Reformed confession that says tradition is authoritative. How then can he claim that this is the "historic Protestant position"? Furthermore, Wilson fails to tell us which traditions of "the Church" are authoritative and which are not. The Marian tradition? The tradition that Christ's body is ubiquitous? The tradition that holds there are more than 66 books in the Bible? The Apocryphal tradition? Does he intend to say that all tradition, with all its contradictions and errors, is authoritative? If not, then he must tell us which traditions are true and which are false. In order to do that he must use a standard that is not a tradition. Wilson, of course, does not tell us which traditions are authoritative because he cannot. Distinguishing authoritative traditions from non-authoritative traditions (if there is any) would require some standard by which traditions are judged. And that standard, not the tradition, then becomes the sole authority. In Romanism, the standard is the Church: *sola Ecclesia*. In Christianity, the standard is the Scripture: *sola Scriptura*. And Wilson denies *sola Scriptura* and exalts the Church.

Furthermore, Wilson's position implies another absurd conclusion: The traditions of the Church, which may be wrong (they are not infallible, he says) are nonetheless "authoritative." This is the same position on church tradition – it is both authoritative and fallible – that many so-called scholars take on the Scriptures. One must ask of Wilson, as we ask of them, what epistemic authority does error have? Why are we obliged to believe something that might be false?

Equally insidious is Wilson's distinction between the "interpretive authority" of creeds and the "ultimate authority" of Scripture. This is similar to the teaching of the Roman Church-State, which, as the self-proclaimed divine keeper of both Scripture and tradition, claims to have the sole "interpretive authority." The Roman Church-State is the authoritative interpreter of Scripture (so it says), because it wrote and approved the Bible, and it is the repository of all authoritative traditions not written in the Bible. Both the Roman Catholic view and Wilson's view of authoritative tradition eliminate the "ultimate authority" of Scripture by placing Scripture in an unknowable realm.

They both admit that Scripture is "authoritative," but what Scripture means must determined by the Church using "tradition." It cannot be determined by Scripture interpreting Scripture. In neither Romanism nor Wilsonism is Scripture *per se* the authority, for Scripture-as-it-is is unavailable to us. Only Scripture-as-interpreted-by-tradition is available to us. Wilson's and Rome's denial of "mere Scripture" in their doctrines of knowledge lays the foundation for their denials of "mere belief of Scripture" in their doctrines of salvation.

Wilson makes this clear: "God has created us in such a way that we do not have the luxury of a 'no tradition' option" (51). Divine revelation must always, according to Wilson, be filtered through tradition. We cannot know God's Word directly or immediately. We can know Scripture only as it appears to us through tradition, the uninspired words of men. In Wilson's theology, tradition is the Kantian barrier (the Dooyeweerdian Boundary) that blocks our direct access to the Word of God. The alternative that Wilson conveniently forgot to mention in his taxonomy of tradition – that tradition is neither absolute nor authoritative – he here explicitly denies. He had asserted that we must choose one of three views, all of which make tradition authoritative or absolute. Contradicting Scripture and the *Westminster Confession*, Wilson says that it is impossible to accept Scripture alone as our authority. Of course, Wilson also says he favors *sola Scriptura*. This is disingenuous. Wilson opposes the Reformers on the crucial principle of the Reformation: Scripture alone. They stated, in Latin (which Wilson loves to use), the principle that Scripture interprets itself: *Scripturam ex Scriptura explicandam esse*: Scripture is to be explained from Scripture. They said this so often, they emphasized it so much, that it became a bumper sticker slogan for the carts and carriages of sixteenth- and seventeenth-century Christians. To claim, as Wilson does, that one is defending the original intent of the Reformers while denying this principle is subreption.

The Session at Christ Church in Moscow, Idaho, responded to the RPCUS' "Call for Repentance" by stating that "Douglas Wilson...holds to the historic Reformed faith as represented by the Westminster Standards on such questions as justification by a faith that is never alone (11:2), and the real presence of the body and blood of Christ in the Lord's Supper to worthy receivers (29:7)." Like so much else in Wilson's book, this statement is disingenuous and deceptive, and the Session knows or should know that it is misrepresenting what the *Confession* says on these matters, and obscuring what Wilson believes. The Session asserts half-truths that are wholly misleading. The question is not whether Wilson holds to this or that point of the "historic Reformed faith as represented by the Westminster Standards" (even while artfully misrepresenting those Standards), but whether or not his opinions contradict or undermine the system of truth summarized in those Standards and taught in the Scriptures. Christianity is a logical, propositional system, not an aggregate of disjointed thoughts and metaphors; and Wilson's dislike of logical systems, propositions, and of logic itself, is well known. Wilson is opposed to all systems, especially theological systems. He is even opposed to arithmetic.[18] His agreement with one or two points in the *Confession* (if in fact he does agree) does not make him Reformed. But, as a matter of fact, Wilson does not agree with the *Confession* even on these two points, as we shall see.

18. In 1999 Wilson published an essay titled "The Great Logic Fraud" in his book *The Paideia of God*. It expresses his revolt against excellence, precision, and logic. That essay belies any claim Wilson might make to believe the system of truth in the *Westminster Confession*. In the essay, Wilson even denies that 2 + 2 = 4 is true. His exact words are, for those who might find my accusation incredible, "Because of our realist assumptions in mathematics, we have come to believe that 15 + 20 = 35 is true. But it is evidently not true" (85).

6. The "Objectivity" of the Covenant

Wilson's overriding concern, as his book's subtitle shows, is recovering the "objectivity" of the covenant. Unfortunately, he does not tell us when the covenant was "objective," and so can be "recovered," nor when it became subjective. But it is clear what he means by "objectivity": He means "photograph-ability," visibility. Throughout the book he denigrates the "ethereal," the "invisible." This is most unfortunate, for a covenant is invisible. A covenant is an agreement; the Covenant of Grace is a divine promise to the elect, and a promise is a proposition. A sign of a covenant, such as baptism, or a rainbow, is visible (that is why it is called a "sign"), but a sign is not the covenant. Wilson's attempt "to recover" – the correct verb would be "to invent" – a visible covenant is not only an attempt to draw a square circle, it is a repudiation of God's Covenant with Christ and his people. There is no Reformed confession that describes the Covenant of Grace as "objective." The objective covenant is a fiction that Wilson has invented.

Here is how God, but not Wilson, describes the Covenant of Grace, in both Old and New Testaments:

> Behold the days are coming, says the Lord, when I will make a new covenant with the house of Israel and with the house of Judah – not according to the covenant that I made with their fathers in the day that I took them by the hand to bring them out of the land of Egypt [the Mosaic covenant].... But this is the covenant that I will make with the house of Israel after those days, says the Lord: I will put my law in their minds, and write it on their hearts; and I will be their God, and they shall be my people. No more shall every man teach his neighbor, and every man his brother, saying "Know the Lord," for they all shall know me, from the least of them to the

> greatest of them, says the Lord. For I will forgive their iniquity, and their sin I will remember no more [*Jeremiah* 31:31-34].

Notice that God says, "this is the covenant," and immediately defines the covenant as a proposition: "I will put my law in their minds, and write it on their hearts; and I will be their God, and they shall be my people." That promise is God's Covenant of Grace. By reducing the promise to writing, the proposition is accurately represented by Hebrew or English letters, but the proposition, the promise, remains invisible. The proposition is intellectual, and Wilson despises the intellect. He prefers sensory titillation; hence his demand for a square circle: a photographable covenant.

And here is the Covenant of Grace from the New Testament:

> But now he [Jesus Christ] has obtained a more excellent ministry, inasmuch as he is also Mediator of a better covenant, which was established on better promises. For if the first covenant [mediated by Moses] had been faultless, then no place would have been sought for a second. Because finding fault with them, he says, "Behold, the days are coming, says the Lord, when I will make a new covenant with the house of Israel and with the house of Judah – not according to the covenant that I made with their fathers in the day when I took them by the hand to lead them out of the land of Egypt; because they did not continue in my covenant, and I disregarded them, says the Lord. For this is the covenant that I will make with the house of Israel after those days, says the Lord: I will put my laws in their mind and write them in their hearts; and I will be their God, and they shall be my people. None of them shall teach his neighbor, and none his brother, saying, 'Know the Lord,' for all shall know me, from the least of them to the greatest of them. For I will

> be merciful to their unrighteousness, and their sins and their lawless deeds I will remember no more." In that he says, "a new covenant," he has made the first [Mosaic covenant] obsolete. Now what is becoming obsolete and growing old is ready to vanish away [*Hebrews* 8:6-13].

In these passages God describes his Covenant of Grace in terms Wilson foolishly rejects: The Covenant of Grace is *invisible*, propositions written in the invisible *minds* of his people; it is a promise made to *individuals*, for only individuals have *minds* in which the Covenant can be written; and the Covenant is *unphotographable.* Wilson is an earthy, sensate man; what he describes as "objective" are things he can see, point at, and photograph. Everything else is "ethereal." Wilson demands an "objective" covenant, that is, a covenant that can be photographed. I enclose Wilson's word "objective" in quotation marks, for God's invisible Covenant of Grace *is* objective, despite what Wilson says. Wilson's sensualistic epistemology requires him to say that visible things are objective and invisible things are not. Of course, that makes God, truth, justice, righteousness, faith – none of which is visible and photographable – ethereal and non-objective. By imposing an un-Biblical theory of knowledge on Scripture, Wilson is inventing another, Antichristian theology, using Christian terminology.[19]

19. Oddly, in one of the book's last chapters ("Covenant Succession," 22), Wilson derides the demand for visible conversions in colonial New England: "Everyone had to be 'born again' in a highly visible, demonstrable way..." (184). Because of comments like this, one begins to suspect that Wilson's demand for visibility is really an expression of his desire for another way of salvation, apart from being born again. He wants a way of salvation that authorized representatives of a photographable Church control, not one that the invisible Holy Spirit controls.

7. What Is a Christian?

Wilson redefines basic Christian terms, and one of the terms he redefines is "Christian." He uses the word in the same way that people who cannot tell the difference between Protestantism, Romanism, and Liberalism use the word: inaccurately and equivocally. Just as infants call every adult male they see "Daddy," Wilson calls every baptized man he sees "Christian." Wilson even has the audacity to argue that this infantile meaning is the "New Testament sense" (14). He writes: "This question [what is a Christian?] is one of the most important questions a man can ask himself. Tied in with it are all the related questions about God, man, sin, salvation, and revelation" (14). Wilson lets us know that by redefining this word, he is simultaneously re-structuring all other doctrines. Please keep that in mind as we examine what he says.

Wilson cites three verses – *Acts* 11:26, *Acts* 26:28; *1 Peter* 4:16 – and from these three he concludes that a Christian is anyone who has been baptized. Here are his words: "A Christian…is anyone who has been baptized in the name of the Father, Son and Holy Spirit by an authorized representative of the Christian church" (19). It follows from this, he says, that "Membership in the Christian faith is objective – it can be photographed and fingerprinted" (21). It is not something invisible, such as faith, or regeneration, or effectual calling, that makes one a Christian, but something visible: baptism by "an authorized representative of the Christian church."

Before we unpack the implications of his statement, we must ask: How does Wilson get that conclusion from these three verses? As a matter of fact, he doesn't, for the verses say no such thing. Here is what they do say:

Now those who were scattered after the persecution that arose over Stephen traveled as far as Phoenicia, Cyprus, and Antioch, preaching the Word to none but the Jews only. But some of them were men from Cyprus and Cyrene, who, when they had come to Antioch, spoke to the Hellenists, preaching the Lord Jesus. And the hand of the Lord was with them, and a great number believed and turned to the Lord.

The news of these things came to the ears of the church in Jerusalem, and they sent out Barnabas to go as far as Antioch. When he came and had seen the grace of God, he was glad, and encouraged them all that with purpose of heart they should continue with the Lord. For he was a good man, full of the Holy Spirit and of faith. And a great many people were added to the Lord.

Then Barnabas departed for Tarsus to seek Saul. And when he had found him, he brought him to Antioch. So it was that for a whole year they assembled with the church and taught a great many people. And the disciples were first called Christians in Antioch [*Acts* 11:19-26].

"Therefore, King Agrippa, I [Paul] was not disobedient to the heavenly vision, but declared first to those in Damascus and in Jerusalem, and throughout all the region of Judea, and then to the Gentiles, that they should repent, turn to God, and do works befitting repentance. For these reasons the Jews seized me in the temple and tried to kill me. Therefore, having obtained help from God, to this day I stand, witnessing both to small and great, saying no other things than those which the prophets and Moses said would come – that the Christ would suffer, that he would be the first to rise from the dead, and would proclaim light to the Jewish people and to the Gentiles."

Now as he [Paul] thus made his defense, Festus said

> with a loud voice, "Paul, you are beside yourself! Much learning is driving you mad!"
>
> But he [Paul] said, "I am not mad, most noble Festus, but speak the words of truth and reason. For the King, before whom I also speak freely, knows these things; for I am convinced that none of these things escapes his attention, since this thing was not done in a corner. King Agrippa, do you believe the prophets? I know that you do believe."
>
> Then Agrippa said to Paul, "You almost persuade me to become a Christian."
>
> And Paul said, "I would to God that not only you, but also all who hear me today, might become both almost and altogether such as I am, except for these chains" [*Acts* 26:28].

> If you are reproached for the name of Christ, blessed are you, for the Spirit of glory and of God rests upon you. On their part he is blasphemed, but on your part he is glorified. But let none of you suffer as a murderer, a thief, an evildoer, or as a busybody in other people's matters. Yet if anyone suffers as a Christian, let him not be ashamed, but let him glorify God in this matter [*1 Peter* 4:14-16].

From these verses Wilson concludes that "the first usage in the Bible [*Acts* 11:26] is a simple reference to what the followers of Christ came to be called – by outsiders." The verse, as the reader can see, does not say that.[20] Please read it – in fact, read the whole chapter – again. Wilson expatiates on what the "pa-

20. There is no Biblical evidence for the assertion that the word *Christian* was invented by unbelievers as a term of reproach. Furthermore, the term *Christian* would not have been received as a reproach by any genuine believer. Some commentators, including some much better than Wilson, have allowed themselves to be swayed by what Wilson calls "very nebulous and unexamined oral traditions" (52).

gans at Antioch" did – all without citing a scintilla of Biblical evidence for his remarks. This is a textbook example of eisegesis, and it is a pattern that Wilson repeats throughout his book. Wilson has imposed on Scripture something it simply does not say. He asserts his opinion without quoting even a non-Biblical source for his opinion.

Furthermore, the Biblical text *does* say that the Antiochans heard the "preaching" of the "Word," "believed," "turned to the Lord," were "disciples," were "added to the Lord" (a phrase that means united to Christ), and thus "Christians," because they were "taught" and "believed" the Word, not because they were baptized. The passage mentions teaching, preaching, and believing; it does not mention baptizing. Only doctrine, not sacrament, is mentioned. Wilson ignores the text completely.

As Luke explains in chapter 11, the number of believers in Antioch had grown very quickly, and Barnabas, sent from the Jerusalem church to help the believers in Antioch, could not do all the teaching necessary in order to obey Christ's command to teach them all things that he had taught. That is why Barnabas left Antioch to go Tarsus to find Paul and bring him back to help teach the new Christians in Antioch. An attentive reading of *Acts* 11 shows that all these people became Christians in only one way: by believing the Gospel of Jesus Christ. Consider these verses:

> 1. The apostles and brethren who were in Judea heard that the Gentiles had also received the Word of God...
>
> 14. ...[Peter] will tell you words by which you and all your household will be saved.
>
> 17. ...God gave them [Gentiles] the same gift as he gave us when we believed in the Lord Jesus Christ...
>
> 19. ...preaching the Word...

20. ...preaching the Lord Jesus...
21. ...a great number believed and turned to the Lord.

The only mention of water baptism in the chapter is found in verse 16, which unfavorably contrasts water baptism to baptism with the Holy Spirit – regeneration: "Then I [Peter] remembered the word of the Lord, how he said, 'John indeed baptized you with water, but you shall be baptized with the Holy Spirit.'" There is no hint anywhere in this chapter or in the entire Bible that people were called Christians because they had been baptized with water. All the textual evidence points to the fact that they were called Christians because they had believed the Gospel of Jesus Christ which had been preached to them. Luke says that it was the "disciples" – he does not say it was the "baptized" – who were called Christians in Antioch. The Greek word "disciple" (*mathētēs*) is derived from the verb "to learn" *(manthano)*. It refers to anyone who seeks knowledge, for a disciple is a learner. The term Luke uses clearly indicates that what distinguished these Antiochans from other Antiochans was intellectual activity – understanding and believing the Gospel – not ritual activity.

Calvin's comments on this verse are both informative and contradictory to Wilson's unsupported speculations:

> He [Luke] added afterward, that such a holy concord [at Antioch] was blessed from Heaven, for this was no small honor that the holy name of Christians began there for all the world. Though the apostles had been a long time at Jerusalem, yet God had not vouchsafed [granted] to bestow upon his Church, which was there, this excellent title of his Son.... And what is it to be a disciple of Christ but to be a Christian? But when they began plainly to be called that which they were, the use of the name served greatly to set forth the glory of Christ, because by

> this means they referred all their religion unto Christ alone. This was, therefore, a most excellent worship for the city of Antioch, that Christ brought forth his name thence, like a standard, whereby it might be made known to all the world that there was some people whose captain was Christ, and which did glory in his name.

The eighteenth-century Baptist theologian John Gill wrote:

> Whether this name of "Christians," which comes from Christ, and signifies anointed ones, was given by their enemies or their friends, by others, or themselves, is not certain, though it is most likely the latter; and it may be they hit upon this general appellation...and so happily buried the distinction of Jews and Gentiles, or those of the circumcision that believed, and those of the uncircumcision.... John of Antioch gives an account of this matter in these words: "at the beginning of the reign of Claudius Caesar, ten years after Jesus Christ, our Lord and God, was ascended up into Heaven, Euodus, the first after the Apostle Peter, being chosen bishop of Antioch, the great city of Syria, became patriarch and under him they were called Christians; for this same bishop, Euodus, conferring with them, put this name upon them, whereas before the Christians were called Nazarenes and Galileans."

The source that Gill cites – and Wilson cites no source for his opinion that the term "Christians" was coined by pagans – says that the name was what the Christians at Antioch called themselves.

Wilson further asserts that in using the word "Christian," "No statement was being made about the great questions mentioned above [God, man, sin, salvation, and revelation] as they might have applied to an individual member of that church [at Antioch]" (14-15). This also is unsupported and contradicted by the text. The several "disciples," the Holy Spirit says, were called "Christians," plural. The text does not say, "The corporate church was called Christian," but that the "disciples," individuals, plural, were called "Christians," plural. The name was applied to individual believers. They were individuals who were taught the Gospel and who believed the Gospel. But Wilson is determined – no matter what the Bible says – to make the word "Christian" refer to a collective, to assign it promiscuously to a visible aggregation of baptized people; for he wants to deny that a Christian is an individual who has believed the words by which he may be saved, as *Acts* says. In Wilson's theology the institutional church – the Holy Hive – has primacy, and the individual person is of secondary importance. In Wilson's theology, "becoming or being a Christian" is a derivative concept – derivative from the visible collective of which one is a member by virtue of ritual baptism performed by "an authorized representative of the Christian church" – rather than by virtue of an invisible ("ethereal" is the derogatory word he uses throughout the book) act of the Holy Spirit writing God's Word in the mind of the believer. Wilson, as at least a semi-devout medievalist, believes in the primacy of the visible, photographable collective, which he calls the "church." Wilson does not believe in the primacy of truth, nor of the individual soul, nor of persons, who by reason of their God-given belief are Christians, savingly united directly (without the mediation of church, priest, or ritual) to Christ by belief alone, and as a consequence of being directly united with the Head, are members of Christ's body.

Wilson further asserts that in Paul's preaching of the Gospel to King Agrippa in *Acts* 26, "even here there is no distinction made between a false profession of Christ and a true profession of Christ" (15). Once again, this is false, and not only false, but preposterous. But before looking again at the text itself, we must ask, Why does Wilson even make this assertion that the text makes no distinction between a true and a false profession of Christ? The answer is that in Wilson's theology, all who *profess* Christ, all who are baptized, not all who *believe* Christ, are "Christians." In his theology, it makes no difference if their profession is true or false; whether they are hypocrites or sincere, whether they are false or true: What is in their hearts is invisible and therefore not objective. Their profession is visible (or at least audible), and, most important of all, their baptism is visible, and that is what makes them Christians. According to Wilson, all who *are baptized* are Christians, and the word *Christian* is properly applied to them. It is not properly applied only to believers of the Gospel. Later in the book Wilson will deny that there is any such thing as a "nominal Christian" – that is, a Christian in name only. He asserts that all baptized persons without exception are properly called Christians, and that this is the only way the Bible uses the word "Christian."

Now, back to the Biblical text, and to the question of whether it makes a distinction between a true and false profession of Christ. In *Acts* 26:24, Festus accuses Paul of being beside himself. Paul denies it, and asserts that his profession is true: "I am not mad, most noble Festus, but speak the words of truth and reason." Paul asserts that he is making a true profession, that he is not deceived, or lying, or mad. Wilson denies this, even while quoting Paul's explicit denial that he is speaking falsehood and his explicit assertion that he is speaking "words of truth and reason." Because of his antipathy toward reason, Wilson ignores this, and the meaning of the following verse as well. There seems to be a veil over Wilson's eyes as he reads this and other passages of Scripture, for Scripture repeatedly contradicts what he asserts.

In his response to Paul's testimony and argument, Agrippa

says, "You almost persuade me to become a Christian." Persuasion is an intellectual activity, and "becoming a Christian" – "coming to the knowledge of the truth," as Paul puts it in *1 Timothy* 2:4 – involves the intellect as much as solving a problem in arithmetic. Becoming a Christian is not the result of a ritual, nor is it a ritual activity itself, nor is it a corporate activity. Becoming a Christian, because it is "coming to the knowledge of the truth," is always intellectual and always individual. Each man must understand and believe the truth for himself. It is impossible for one person to understand and believe for another. Belief is a gift the Holy Spirit gives to those for whom Christ died. The Holy Spirit does not understand or believe for them; he causes them to understand and believe the truth. That gift is dispensed only to individuals, one individual at a time, by the direct and immediate activity of the Spirit on their minds. Individual minds – and individual minds are the only minds there are – are enlightened by the Holy Spirit, the Spirit of Truth. Scripture refers to this activity as "regeneration," "resurrection," "illumination," and, more literally, "coming to the knowledge of the truth." Wilson's theology actually attacks this divine enlightenment, this Spiritual illumination. Rather than opposing the eighteenth-century Enlightenment, Wilson apes one of its leading figures, Immanuel Kant, and denigrates the work of the Holy Spirit in bringing individual souls to the knowledge of the truth. One does not become a Christian by heritage, birth, or baptism: "But as many as received him to them he gave the right to become children of God, even to those who believe in his name: who were born, not of blood, nor of the will of the flesh, nor of the will of man, but of God" (*John* 1:12-13). It is belief alone that confers on sinners the right to be called children of God.

Wilson writes: "In all three places [in Scripture], the word ["Christian"] is used by pagans" (16). Wilson's assertion would imply that the Apostle Peter is a pagan, since he wrote, "If any man suffer as a Christian." And Wilson repeats his errors: "In Antioch, the pagans call the Christians by this name. In Paul's hearing, Agrippa speaks it in his summary of what he thinks Paul was trying to do to him. [By saying "what he thinks Paul was trying to do to him," Wilson makes Agrippa sound suspicious of Paul's intentions, but the text gives no evidence of such suspicion, and Agrippa was a sympathetic hearer of Paul who would have freed him, had Paul not appealed to Caesar.– JR & SG] In the passage from Peter, an apostle imputes a hatred of the name of Christ, and this use of the word *Christian*, to pagan persecutors" (16-17). Once again, Wilson's overheated imagination twists what the text actually says. So far is Peter from "imput[ing]...this use of the word *Christian* to pagan persecutors" that Peter owns the word as accurate and honorable, and equates it with the "name of Christ." "Suffering as a Christian" is the same as "suffering for the name of Christ"[21] and it is something to be gloried in, not ashamed of, Peter says.

From his baseless interpretation of this passage Wilson draws another conclusion: "And this means that we have no distinctively Christian handling of the word *Christian*" in Scripture (17). Here we pause to let Wilson's words sink in. Wilson does not notice, as we hope the reader does, that this conclusion destroys his argument: If it is the case that "we have no distinctively Christian handling of the word *Christian*" in Scripture, then Wilson's whole argument collapses. Why are Christians obliged to use a word – which Wilson says was coined, defined, and used exclusively and pejoratively by pagans – in the same way pagans used it? If "we have no distinctively Christian handling of the word *Christian*" in Scripture, then Wilson

21. See *Matthew* 10:22; 19:29; 24:9; *Mark* 13:13; *Luke* 21:12, 17; *John* 15:21.

cannot validly argue that the pagan usage merely reported in Scripture is the proper meaning of the word.

But, contrary to Wilson, it is not true that "we have no distinctively Christian handling of the word *Christian*" in Scripture. Wilson, in the space of a few lines, has forgotten Peter's statement, as well as Paul's tacit approval of Agrippa's use of the word (Paul does not correct Agrippa or even demur, but accepts the name "Christian" as accurate and honorable), as well as what the disciples in Antioch called themselves. They were all disciples of Christ: *Christians.*

Wilson then makes this assertion: "Here [in a typical "evangelical" account of conversion] 'becoming a Christian' means passing from one spiritual state to another, from darkness to light. It refers to conversion as an internal reality, *but the Bible does not apply the word Christian to this or describe the process as that of becoming a Christian*" (17, emphasis added). Let's assume for a moment that Wilson's statement is correct. What follows? What can we deduce from it? Wilson has just told us that all the Bible is doing when it uses the word "Christian" is reporting how pagans used the word. The Bible is not giving us a Christian definition, he says. So why should we be required to use the word "Christian" as pagans did?

We have emphasized the last part of Wilson's sentence, for it indicates where Wilson is taking us. According to Wilson, the "New Testament sense" of the word *Christian* is *not* "believer" or "disciple," and "becoming a Christian" is *not* "passing from one spiritual state to another, from darkness to light." But the Bible does precisely what Wilson denies: It calls those who have been taught the Gospel, who have heard and believed the words of eternal life, those who have passed from death to life, *Christians* – see *Acts* 11. The Apostle Peter calls believers "Christians" – see *1 Peter*. Paul urges Agrippa to believe his statements, his propositions, just as he believes the

Old Testament prophets (see verse 27); Paul does not urge Agrippa to undergo ritual baptism in order to become a Christian. Paul describes his mission in these words: "to open their eyes and to turn them from darkness to light, and from the power of Satan to God, that they may receive forgiveness of sins and an inheritance among those who are sanctified by faith in me" (*Acts* 26:18). This is an inward, invisible change – for which Wilson asserts it is improper to use the phrase "become a Christian." Paul's words, "sanctified by faith in me"; Peter's words, "come to the knowledge of the truth"; Christ's words, "You must be born again" – contradict Wilson's theology, for he wants something visible, ritual baptism, to distinguish Christians from non-Christians; and regeneration, faith, sanctification, and coming to the knowledge of the truth are not visible.

Paul made clear what his mission was and what becoming a Christian means when he wrote:

> Christ did not send me to baptize, but to preach the Gospel, not with wisdom of words, lest the cross of Christ should be made of no effect, for the message of the cross is foolishness to those who are perishing, but to us who are being saved it is the power of God.... For since, in the wisdom of God, the world through wisdom did not know God, it pleased God through the foolishness of the message preached to save those who believe [*1 Corinthians* 1:17-21].

Paul makes it clear (1) that his sole purpose, given to him by Christ, is to preach the Gospel, not to baptize; (2) that only by hearing the Gospel men are saved; (3) that the Gospel is not wisdom that men originated, but words revealed by God; (4) that the words of the Gospel are powerful; and (5) that those saved are those who believe the Gospel, not those who are baptized.

In his Vantilian double-mindedness, Wilson paraphrases *Romans* 2:28-29: "For he is not a Christian who is one outwardly; neither is that baptism, which is outward and external. But he is a Christian who is one inwardly; and baptism is that of the heart, in the spirit, and not in the letter..." (18). Exactly. But Wilson immediately adds, "Paul's statement was hyperbolic." He argues that "they were of course Jews in another [sense]." Of course, they were Jews in the sense that they were physical descendants of Abraham, but Paul says that sense is religiously insignificant: "He is not a Jew who is one outwardly." Since Wilson made the paraphrase, substituting the word "Christian" for "Jew," and the word "baptism" for "circumcision," we must ask, To what does he think Jewish physical descent corresponds in Christians? Is Wilson suggesting that because parents are Christians, their baptized children also are Christians? He is more than suggesting that, he is asserting it explicitly, and Paul here, in Wilson's own paraphrase, explicitly denies it. *John* 1:12-13 also deny it: "But as many as received him [Jesus Christ], to them he gave the right to become children of God, to those who believe in his name" – notice that John defines "receive" as "believe." John does not say, "But as many as received him, to them he gave the right to become children of God, to those who are baptized in his name." John says "believe," an invisible, intellectual act that can be performed only by an individual. Wilson's theology is not John's. In verse 13 John continues the thought: "who [those who believe in his name] were born, not of blood, nor of the will of the flesh, nor of the will of man, but of God." Let me be perfectly clear: A godly heritage saves no one. Having Christian parents saves no one. Being baptized saves no one. All these things actually condemn a person more severely, if the person so privileged does not believe the Gospel.[22] The only thing that gives a person the right to become a child of God is being "born of God," the invisible act that God accomplishes directly and immediately in the mind of the sinner, the sort of ethereal act at which Wilson sneers.

Because he does not understand the Covenant of Grace, Wilson employs a new term for people who he says are "unbelieving Christians": They are, he says, "covenantal Christians." By this phrase, Wilson indicates his rejection of the Covenant of Grace, for in that Covenant, as God explained in *Jeremiah* and *Hebrews*, there is no such thing as a covenantal, unbelieving Christian: "All shall know me, from the least to the greatest of them." A "covenantal Christian," if one uses the word "covenant" as the Bible uses it, is a redundancy. This shows that Wilson is using the word "covenant" in a way different from the way the Bible uses it. If one believes the covenant is "visible," as Wilson does, the phrase "covenantal Christian" changes the meaning of both "covenant" and "Christian." In Wilson's Antichristian theology, Ishmael, who was circumcised (the Old Testament sign of the covenant and analogue of baptism), was also in the covenant, even though God had said that Ishmael was not in the covenant:

> And as for Ishmael, I have heard you [Abraham]. Behold, I have blessed him [Ishmael], and will make him fruitful, and will multiply him exceedingly. He shall beget twelve princes, and I will make him a great nation. *But my Covenant I will establish with Isaac* [not with Ishamel]..." [*Genesis* 17:21].

In Wilson's theology, though not in Christian theology, bearing the sign of the covenant makes one a member of the

22. This is Paul's argument about the Jews in *Romans* 2: They are more severely condemned because of their greater privileges and knowledge.

covenant. Ishmael was circumcised, but God made the covenant only with Isaac. God denies the "objectivity" of his Covenant of Grace in *Genesis* 17, as well as *Romans* 9.

The phrase "covenantal Christian," Wilson assures us, "does show that the word *Christian* can be used in two senses" (19). Now, if this were in fact his point, Wilson could have saved himself and his readers a lot of trouble by simply quoting a good dictionary. We have before us the *Oxford English Dictionary*. Under the word "Christian" it gives several meanings:

> (1) believing, professing or belonging to the religion of Christ;
>
> (2) pertaining to Christ or his religion: of or belonging to Christianity;
>
> (3) showing character and conduct consistent with discipleship to Christ: marked by genuine piety; following the precepts and example of Christ: Christ-like;
>
> (4) humane as distinguished from brutal;
>
> (5) civilized; decent, respectable;
>
> (6) one who believes or professes the religion of Christ; an adherent of Christianity;
>
> (7) one who exhibits the spirit and follows the precept and example of Christ: a believer in Christ who is characterized by genuine piety;
>
> (8) a human being as distinguished from a brute;
>
> (9) a denominational or sectarian name;
>
> (10) a variety of pear;
>
> (11) a variety of plum;
>
> (12) verb: to make Christian, to christen.

Merriam-Webster's adds a few more meanings, including "the hero in Bunyan's *Pilgrim's Progress*." So here we have a baker's dozen of uses of the word "Christian." So what?

It is *not* Wilson's point that "the word *Christian* can be used in two senses." That is trivial, and he is being disingenuous.

His point – for which there is no Biblical support – is twofold: (1) the Bible uses the word "Christian" to mean someone who has been baptized or who professes – whether truly or falsely does not matter – merely professes to be a disciple of Christ; and (2) the Bible *never* uses the word "Christian" to refer only to one who is a born-again believer of the Gospel. We have shown above that both these assertions are false, and Wilson supplies no Biblical text to support either one. He wants his readers to accept – right in chapter 1 – his assertion that the Bible uses the word "Christian" in its proper sense to refer to all baptized persons. If he can get his readers to accept that redefinition of the word "Christian," he thinks he can get them to accept everything else he has to say about "God, man, sin, salvation, and revelation." Without that redefinition of the word "Christian," the rest of his book has no plausibility whatever. With it, he can more easily pretend that his medieval theology is the "historic Reformed faith." Wilson commits the very error he warns his readers against on page 54: "systematic interpretations may be allowed to *interpret* what the Scriptures say..., but they must never be allowed to *replace* what the Scriptures say." Wilson has replaced what the Scriptures say about Christians with his own meaning for the word, for his medieval theology requires it.

Let us examine the way Wilson uses, and wants us to use, the word "Christian": "a Christian is anyone who has been baptized in the name of the Father, Son and Holy Spirit by an authorized representative of the Christian church" (19). What does this definition accomplish? Several things. First, Wilson's definition falsely identifies ritual baptism as the distinguishing characteristic of Christians. There is no Scriptural support for this whatsoever, as we have just seen. According to Wilson's definition, it is not belief of the Gospel that distinguishes Christians from non-Christians, but having undergone a sacramental rite.[23] Second, Wilson's definition gives "authorized representatives of the Christian church" a monopoly on making Christians. This is sacerdotalism, an Antichristian system in which "authorized representatives of the Christian church" are mediators between God and man. (Later in his book Wilson will discuss sacerdotalism, which he hopelessly confuses with sacramentalism.[24]) Using Wilson's definition of "Christian," only "authorized representatives of the Christian church" can make Christians. One cannot become a Christian by direct action of the Holy Spirit on one's mind. That, Wilson says scornfully, is "refried gnosticism" in which the Holy Spirit uses an "invisible conduit from God to man" to save people (86).[25] One cannot become a Christian while conversing with a neighbor or friend about the Gospel, or even while listening to a sermon. The ritual action of an "authorized representative of the Christian church" is required to become a Christian. Third, because Wilson apparently includes within the "Christian church" any organization that claims the name – remember, he says it makes no difference if

23. Later in the book Wilson will attempt to argue that the rite alone is not effective, but requires other saving graces as well, but in chapter 1 he makes it clear that the invisible things (which he belittles), such as regeneration and faith, are not what make a Christian, but visible baptism (which is "objective"). He wants to have it both ways.

24. Wilson writes, for example "Baptism and salvation are not mechanically or magically linked. But in the ordinary course of life, they *are* linked, and we are to speak of them as though they are. And to do so is *not* sacerdotalism" (87). Of course it is not sacerdotalism, for "sacerdotalism" means "the religious belief emphasizing the powers of priests as essential mediators between God and man." Wilson doesn't know the difference between "sacerdotalism" and "sacramentalism," which is the word he should have used. "Sacramentalism" is the "belief that the sacraments are inherently efficacious and necessary for salvation." Wilson believes this, and he is a sacramentalist. Incidentally, he is also a sacerdotalist, for only "authorized representatives of the Christian church" can perform the sacrament of baptism. In Wilson's theology, priests are indispensable mediators between God and man (sacerdotalism), and sacraments make one a Christian (sacramentalism).

25. This blasphemous statement is an attack on the baptism of the Holy Spirit referred to in *Acts* 11:16 and elsewhere. See also *Matthew* 12:31-32.

a profession is sincere or hypocritical – he includes under that rubric such organizations as the Roman Catholic Church-State, the various Orthodox Catholic cults, and Liberal Protestant sects that practice "trinitarian baptism." Fourth, Wilson's definition of the word "Christian" denies the name "Christian" to everyone who believes the Gospel but has not been baptized by "an authorized representative of the Christian church" – the repentant thief on the cross, for example.[26]

Wilson's pagan definition of "Christian" requires him to talk like this: "If someone has been a Christian his whole life, but then comes into the new life that Christ presented to Nicodemus, we can say that he has become a Christian inwardly.... And if we know what we are saying, and we qualify it as Paul did [how did Paul qualify it?], we might even say that he has become a Christian" (20). Wilson wants to have it both ways.

Immediately Wilson offers us an analogy – he is very adept at inventing misleading analogies, and very inept at constructing valid arguments. He writes:

> However, this [a man becoming a Christian inwardly] would be comparable to a man who was married for ten years but was regularly unfaithful, who finally had a real change of heart. After ten years, he might say, as might his wife, that on the day he repented he finally became a husband. And he did – he finally knows what it is all about. But we need to remember that covenantally he was a husband all along, and had all the obligations of marriage [20].

26. Wilson fails to tell his readers how one becomes an "authorized representative of the Christian church," or how to distinguish an authorized representative from an unauthorized representative. This omission is fatal to his scheme, for in order to become a Christian, one must be baptized by someone with the proper ecclesiastical credentials. Does Wilson himself have those credentials? Where and how did he get them?

Let us diagram this analogy to make it clear where the fault lies, especially since this misleading marriage analogy is the dominating analogy in the book. (Wilson seems to think that arguments from analogy are valid arguments, but, sadly for him, they never are. Did he not dislike logic so much, he might have realized this.) Here is what Wilson's analogy looks like:

Philandering husband : faithful husband :: "unbelieving Christian" : believing Christian.

To show it another way:

Philandering husband		"Unbelieving Christian"
———————	::	———————
Faithful husband		Believing Christian

Now, what is wrong with this analogy? Well, more than one thing, but the basic flaw is this: It is based on a false assumption. Wilson assumes that by ritual baptism people are really united, married, to Christ. Such baptized people, he will say later, who are in genuine spiritual union with Christ, may indeed go to Hell. In ritual baptism, which he views as an analogue of a wedding ceremony, the baptized person is wedded to Christ. Water baptism actually makes one (part of) the Bride of Christ, a member of his body, and the recipient of his "saving graces." Notwithstanding all that, one in such "covenantal union" with Christ may indeed go to Hell.

Wilson's assumption (most arguments go wrong right at the beginning) – for which he offers no valid Scriptural argument – is simply false. Ritual baptism does not unite sinners to Christ; belief of the Gospel does. It is those who believe who are "added to the Lord." The *Westminster Shorter Catechism* accurately summarizes Scripture when it says, "The Spirit applies to us the redemption purchased by Christ, by working faith in us, and *thereby* [that is, by faith] uniting us to

Christ in our effectual calling" (Q. 30). Our union with Christ is a legal and intellectual – spiritual and invisible, if you wish – union. "We have the mind of Christ" and "Christ dwells in our hearts by faith." In this Covenant of Grace, which is not Wilson's covenant, God has written his Word in our minds and hearts. This common doctrine – common to Christ and the believer – is what unites us to Christ, not ritual baptism. Sinners become (part of) the Bride of Christ by believing the Gospel, not by being baptized by water.

An "unbelieving Christian," so fundamental to Wilson's scheme, is a contradiction in terms. A Scriptural analogy would look like this:

$$\frac{\text{Fornicator}}{\text{Husband}} :: \frac{\text{Unbeliever}}{\text{Believer}}$$

This analogy would have toppled Wilson's whole theological house of cards, which rests on the central falsehood that all baptized sinners, elect and reprobate, believing and unbelieving, are genuinely, spiritually, wedded to Christ by ritual baptism.

Wilson tells us that there are two errors to avoid: "The first error is that of individualistic pietism, assuming that invisible saints are the only saints, or, rather, that invisible saintliness is the only kind." By using jargon, twice over, and by creating a straw man, Wilson hopes we will agree that all who are visibly baptized are "saints," a proposition for which there is no Scriptural support. Wilson does not (because he cannot) cite a single instance in which Scripture uses the word "saint" to refer to an unbeliever. He simply makes an assertion and expects his readers to believe him. Many of them foolishly do.

The second error to avoid, according to Wilson, is hypocrisy: "This is the idea that mere covenant membership can replace covenant faithfulness as the one thing needful" (21). There are many fatal errors in this simple sentence, and they become obvious in the remainder of the book.

First, Wilson's "objective covenant" is not the Covenant of Grace, and Wilson's "objective covenant" is salvifically useless. One can be a member of Wilson's "objective covenant" and go to Hell, but no member of the Covenant of Grace can go to Hell. Clearly we have before us two different covenants, and Wilson's book is an attempt to substitute his objective covenant for the Covenant of Grace taught in Scripture. By asserting the corporate "objectivity" of his covenant, Wilson has denied its efficacy. Wilson's covenant is not the Covenant of Grace; it is a covenant of works. It does not save its members, but requires them to perform good works in order to be saved or to retain their salvation. That is what Wilson means by "covenantal faithfulness."

Second – and one has to keep both eyes on the pea when reading Wilson, that great shuffler of thimbles – notice that belief – faith – has disappeared entirely from Wilson's objective covenant. Wilson leaves us with only two things: "mere covenant membership" and "covenant faithfulness." The former, while necessary, is not sufficient for salvation, he says. What determines one's salvation is one's own "covenant faithfulness." That is, salvation depends on one's own performance. Keep in mind that "faith" is not synonymous with "faithfulness." By "faithfulness" Wilson means loyalty, obedience, works. In Wilson's theology, salvation is by ritual baptism and good works. This, of course, is essentially the position of the Roman Church-State: Membership in the Church, conferred by ritual baptism performed by an authorized representative of the Church, is necessary for salvation, but it is not sufficient for salvation. In order to be finally saved, the baptized person must also perform satisfactorily.

Third, contrary to Wilson, the "one thing needful" for salvation is not the sinner's covenant faithfulness, but the perfect and meritorious obedience of Christ culminating in his substitutionary death. Christ's perfect righteousness, which is the only righteousness acceptable to God, who is absolutely holy, is imputed to sinners through belief alone. It is Christ's extrinsic righteousness alone that saves sinners, not their alleged covenant faithfulness. Wilson does not understand the "one thing needful," and he denies the Gospel.

One can understand, after Wilson completes his redefinition of the word "Christian" in chapter 1, why he feels compelled to devote the next three chapters to an extended plea for still accepting him as an evangelical and a Calvinist, despite what he has written, and what he will write later in the book. In these chapters he displays further confusion, writing, for example, "if God is the Creator, then He is responsible for the presence of *x* [evil]. We might as well face it" (26). And "What he foreordained was a world full of free choices." Wilson does not bother to tell us what a "free choice" is, nor how free choices are compatible with predestination; and as for God's being "responsible" for anything, that is exactly what Paul denies in *Romans* 9: God cannot be required to give a response to any creature for any of his actions. Wilson should have read – it has been available for 70 years – Dr. Gordon Clark's essay on "Determinism and Responsibility." It might have helped him avoid such Vantilian foolishness as whining: "This makes no sense to some people, but how many basic doctrines do make sense?"

Wilson follows this skeptical question with "We do not understand how God made the solar system from nothing any more than how He determined my actions today without annihilating me. But he did." First, there is no "how" in creation. "How" assumes process, and there can be no process, because there can be no secondary means, in creation *ex nihilo*. So Wilson's question is simply nonsensical. Second, far from annihilating Wilson, God's decree constituted him. He should have known that from reading the Bible. Third, Wilson says "we." He should speak for himself, but Vantilians seem to think that if they cannot understand something, no one can. Dr. Robbins criticized this theological arrogance 20 years ago in a review of George Marston's harmful little book, *The Voice of Authority*.[27]

8. Westminster *versus* Wilson

Throughout these chapters, as well as the rest of the book, Wilson assumes that all who are baptized are "members of the Covenant of Grace." But that is not what Scripture teaches, nor what the Westminster Standards, which Wilson claims to be defending, say. We have already quoted several passages of Scripture on this point, and we shall quote more later. Consider now what the Westminster Standards say: "...the Covenant of Grace: whereby he [God] freely offers unto sinners life and salvation by Jesus Christ, requiring of them faith in him, that they may be saved; and *promising to give unto all those that are ordained unto life his Holy Spirit, to make them willing and able to believe*" (*WCF* 7.3).

Notice that the promise of the Holy Spirit is to "those that are ordained unto eternal life." The promise is not to all men, nor to all who hear the Gospel,[28] nor to all the baptized, nor to all who profess faith, but only to the elect, to "those who are

27. The review is reprinted in *Against the World: The Trinity Review 1978-1988*. The Trinity Foundation, 1996, 26-30.

28. One of the roots of Wilson's medieval religion is the false doctrine of the "free offer of Gospel," in which God is said to desire the salvation of all men, both elect and reprobate, and to offer salvation sincerely to all who hear the Gospel. That doctrine has been a tenet of Vantilianism since its inception.

ordained unto life." Notice also that the promise includes God's making the elect "willing and able to believe." Belief is not a condition that sinners meet in order to receive covenant blessings; *saving faith is itself a promised blessing of the Covenant of Grace*. That is exactly what God says in *Jeremiah* 31 and *Hebrews* 8 when he speaks of writing his Word in the minds of his people. Wilson's misunderstanding – and Norman Shepherd's before him – is that since all the baptized are already in the objective covenant, saving faith cannot be a blessing of the covenant, or all in the objective covenant would have it. Rather than understanding saving faith as a gift that God gives to all members of the Covenant of Grace, they see faith as a condition that covenant members must meet in order to receive the blessings of the covenant. In Wilson's theology, faith is a *quid pro quo*.

The *Confession* continues:

> This covenant [the Covenant of Grace] was differently administered in the time of the law, and in the time of the Gospel; under the law it was administered by promises, prophecies, sacrifices, circumcision, the paschal lamb, and other types and ordinances delivered to the people of the Jews, all foresignifying Christ to come, which were for that time sufficient and efficacious, through the operation of the Spirit, *to instruct and build up the elect in faith in the promised messiah, by whom they had full remission of sins, and eternal salvation....*
>
> ...the grace promised [in baptism] is not only offered, but really exhibited and conferred by the Holy Ghost, *to such (whether of age or infants) as that grace belongs unto*, according to the counsel of God's own will, in his appointed time [*WCF* 28.6].

Once again, only the elect – "such...as that grace belongs unto" – are promised and actually receive grace. There is no promiscuous promise of the Spirit, life, or salvation to all who are baptized, or to all who hear, or to all who profess. Grace and salvation are "promised," "offered," "exhibited," and "conferred" by the Holy Spirit only to those to whom they belong, that is, only to the elect. The notion that salvation is promised to all indiscriminately is a fundamental tenet of Arminianism and Universalism. The notion that God desires the salvation of all men (or even that he desires the salvation of all the baptized) requires Wilson – as it did Norman Shepherd and all Vantilians – to use Arminian language: All hearers (or all the baptized) are promised grace and salvation, but they must meet certain conditions in order to receive them. If they do not meet those conditions, or if they stop meeting those conditions, they lose their justification, salvation, and election.

Furthermore, the *Confession* says, the grace is conferred by the Holy Ghost whenever he pleases. It is not conferred by water baptism, nor by an "authorized representative of the Christian church."

The *Larger Catechism* asks:

> Q. 30 Does God leave all men to perish in the estate of sin and misery?
>
> A. God does not leave all men to perish in the estate of sin and misery, into which they fell by the breach of the first covenant, commonly called the Covenant of Works; but of his mere love and mercy delivers his elect out of it, and brings them into an estate of salvation by the second covenant, commonly called the Covenant of Grace.

Once again, it is the elect alone who are members of Christ, and through him, partakers of the Covenant of Grace.[29] Chapter 8 of the *Westminster Confession* is even more clear:

29. Geerhardus Vos, "The Doctrine of the Covenant in Reformed Theology," *Shorter Writings*, 259, says : "It is equally easy to demonstrate that the [Reformed]

> The Lord Jesus, by his perfect obedience and sacrifice of himself, which he through the eternal Spirit once offered up unto God, has fully satisfied the justice of his Father; and purchased not only reconciliation, but an everlasting inheritance in the kingdom of Heaven *for all those whom the Father has given unto him*.
>
> Although the work of redemption was not actually wrought by Christ till after his incarnation, yet the virtue, efficacy, and benefits thereof, were *communicated unto the elect* in all ages successively from the beginning of the world, in and by those promises, types, and sacrifices, wherein he was revealed and signified to be the Seed of the woman, which should bruise the serpent's head, and the Lamb slain from the beginning of the world, being yesterday and today the same, and forever.
>
> *To all those for whom Christ has purchased redemption*, he does certainly and effectually apply and communicate the same; making intercession *for them*; and revealing *unto them*, in and by the Word, the mysteries of sal-

theologians did not place election and covenant side by side in a dualistic fashion, but related them organically. It is a well-known fact that for many, election circumscribes the extent of the covenant even in their definition of the covenant. This is the case with Witsius, Braun, Lampe, Maestricht, á Marck, á Brakel, Francken and others. One finds this description not only in the later theologians; it is found just as well in the very earliest. Olevianus' work is titled: 'Concerning the Substance of the Covenant of Grace Between God and the Elect.' Szegedin speaks of a 'special and eternal covenant, which God himself deigned to make with the believers and elect' (cited by Heppe, *Geschichte des Pietismus und der Mystik in der Reformirten Kirche*, p. 208). Musculus expressed himself identically, as one can see above. Polanus is no different: 'God made both covenants (old and new) only with the elect'" (*Syntagma*, VI, 33)....

"The covenant of grace has its fixity in God alone, who answers for both parties, and effects man's willing and working by the Holy Spirit. Its fixity does not lie at the end as an ideal to be reached, but in the beginning, in the work of the Mediator, which in turn is already grounded in his eternal guaranty. Hence, it is an unalterable covenant, which extends into eternity. It is an announcement of intended marriage by which the believer is assured of his future." So much for Wilson's ridiculous claim to be defending the original meaning of the Reformers and the *Westminster Confession*.

> vation; effectually *persuading them* by his Spirit to believe and obey; and governing *their hearts* by his Word and Spirit; overcoming all their enemies by his almighty power and wisdom, in such manner and ways as are most consonant to his wonderful and unsearchable dispensation.

The *Larger Catechism* reiterates this doctrine:

> Q. 31 With whom was the Covenant of Grace made?
>
> A. The Covenant of Grace was made with Christ as the second Adam, and *in him with all the elect as his seed.*

Notice that all the elect and only the elect in Christ are mentioned as parties in the Covenant of Grace. They, and only they, are those for whom Christ died. They, and only they, are those whom Christ represented in his life and death. The Covenant of Grace is not made with a mixed multitude of elect and reprobate, nor with the baptized, nor with all members of organized churches.

> Q. 57 What benefits has Christ procured by his mediation?
>
> A. Christ, by his mediation, has procured redemption, with all other benefits of the Covenant of Grace.

Notice that Christ alone procures *all* the benefits, *all the blessings of the Covenant.* They are not procured by the covenant faithfulness of the sinner. Questions 58 and 59 further address the question of who receives the benefits and blessings of Christ's work:

> Q. 58 How do we come to be made partakers of the benefits which Christ has procured?
>
> A. We are made partakers of the benefits which Christ has procured by the application of them unto us, which is the work especially of God the Holy Spirit.

It is not ritual baptism that makes us partakers of the benefits, nor authorized representatives of the Christian church, nor our covenantal faithfulness, but the Holy Spirit alone, who applies them to us by faith alone.

> Q. 59 Who are made partakers of redemption through Christ?
>
> A. Redemption is certainly applied, and effectually communicated, *to all those for whom Christ has purchased it*; who are in time by the Holy Ghost enabled to believe in Christ according to the Gospel.

Notice that "redemption is certainly applied and effectually communicated" to all the elect, here described as "those for whom Christ has purchased it." It is applied to those who believe the Gospel. It is not applied and communicated to all the baptized, nor to all members of organized churches.

The Covenant of Grace does not have a membership list different from God's decree of election. Wilson's ineffective, objective covenant does have a different membership list. Those who are "covenantally elect" in Wilson's theology may very well go to Hell. All they need to do is fail to meet the conditions of the objective covenant. Unfortunately, Wilson fails to tell his readers what the conditions of salvation are and how one knows when one has met them. To refuse to list the conditions of salvation is impolite. To be unable to list the conditions of salvation is disastrous.

In Scripture, there is no difference between those who are "covenantally elect" and those who are "decretally elect," to use Wilson's terms. Such a Kantian distinction – the former knowable because it is in the phenomenal – visible – realm, and the latter unknowable, is completely foreign to Scripture. But it is central to Wilson's theology. This bit of Kantianism shows the influence of the Enlightenment on Wilson's thinking – and he doesn't even realize it.

Wilson does not tell us who the *parties* to his objective covenant are, but he tells us many times who he thinks the "members" are. For example, he tells us that "Nicodemus was a covenant member" (34) even while Christ was telling him, "You must be born again." Obviously neither Nicodemus' "faithful covenant membership" since his circumcision, nor that of his parents, had taken him from darkness into light, nor given him new life, nor resulted in his justification and adoption, for as a circumcised and practicing Jew, Nicodemus could neither see nor enter the kingdom of Heaven.[30] Wilson's objective covenant is an ineffective, external, promiscuous, visible arrangement that bears no resemblance to the effective, internal, selective, and invisible Covenant of Grace.

The parties in the Covenant of Grace are God the Father and Christ the Mediator. The promise of eternal life is to Christ, and to those, and only to those, "chosen by Christ" from before the foundation of the world. The promise is not to all who are baptized, nor to all who profess. By not discussing who the parties to his covenant are, Wilson omits the role of the Mediator from his scheme, eliminates the doctrine of individual election in Christ, and makes all "members" of the covenant personally responsible for fulfilling the conditions of the covenant – on pain of losing their salvation. Wilson's objective covenant is a covenant of works, not the Covenant of Grace.

30. Nicodemus was in fact an elect soul, since he later came to believe the Gospel. But that is not what Wilson means by "covenant membership." According to Wilson, election is invisible, unknowable, and "ethereal"; and circumcision is visible, knowable, and "objective." Wilson means that Nicodemus was a "covenant member" because he was a circumcised Jew, precisely in the same sense as Judas Iscariot. Iscariot's visible faithfulness was such that no one, not even the other disciples, suspected him until after he had betrayed Christ.

The *Larger Catechism* continues:

> Q. 32 How is the grace of God manifested in the second Covenant [the Covenant of Grace]?
>
> A. The grace of God is manifested in the second Covenant, in that he freely provides and offers to sinners a Mediator, and life and salvation by him; and requiring faith as the condition to interest them in him, *promises and gives his Holy Spirit to all his elect, to work in them that faith, with all other saving graces....*

Once again, God the Father promises and gives his Holy Spirit to the elect, and to only the elect. The Holy Spirit, in turn, confers on them all, without exception, faith and all other saving graces. Unlike Wilson's objective covenant, there are no members of the Covenant of Grace who do not receive all saving graces. Here the *Catechism* uses the word "condition," which has been seized upon by the Neolegalists seeking support for their notion of a conditional covenant. But a little reflection will show that this is not what this answer teaches. The *Catechism* here is concerned to show that faith is the only instrument uniting believers to Christ: It speaks of faith as "the condition to interest them in him." Far from teaching some conditional, objective covenant, the *Catechism* here denies that ritual baptism or good works unites sinners to Christ, for faith, not baptism, is "the condition to interest them in him."

Paul was very clear as to whom the promises were made: only to Christ, and those chosen in him, the elect. "Now to Abraham and his seed were the promises made. He says not, and to seeds, as of many, but as of one, and to your seed, which is Christ" (*Galatians* 3:16). The promises are *not* made to all the children of Abraham, *not* to all the circumcised, *not* to all professors of faith, *not* to all those who "make their boast in

God, and know his will, and approve the things that are excellent, being instructed out of the law," and *not* to all those "to whom were committed the oracles of God" (*Romans* 2).

Many of the Jews of Christ's day thought God had made promises of life and salvation to all the children of Abraham, to all the circumcised, just as Wilson imagines that God has made promises of life and salvation to all the children of Christians, to all the baptized. They were wrong then, and Wilson is wrong now. The unbelieving Jews wanted an objective, visible, corporate covenant, and Wilson has an objective, visible, corporate covenant. Neither their imagined covenant nor Wilson's is the Covenant of Grace. Because many of the Jews believed, mistakenly, that God had made promises of life and salvation to all the children of Abraham, they concluded that God had broken his promises to them, because not all of them were saved. Paul is very concerned to answer this attack on the integrity of God, and he does so by pointing out what the Jews should and would have known, had they read their Scriptures with their eyes open:

> But it is not that the Word of God has taken no effect. For they are not all Israel who are of Israel, nor are they all children because they are the seed of Abraham; but "In Isaac [not Ishmael] your seed shall be called." That is, those who are the children of the flesh, these are not the children of God; but the children of the promise are counted as the seed [*Romans* 9:6-8].
>
> God has not cast away his people whom he foreknew.... Even so at this present time there is a remnant according to the election of grace.... Israel has not obtained what it seeks; but the elect have obtained it, and the rest were hardened [*Romans* 11:2, 5, 7].

Paul explains God's faithfulness to his Covenant promises by the doctrine of individual election: God did not break his

Covenant promises to all who are circumcised, because God had made no promises of life and salvation to all who were circumcised. His promises were to the elect, the remnant, only, not to all the children of Abraham. Had God made promises of life and salvation to all the children of Abraham, Isaac, and Jacob (which is how many of the Jews misunderstood the Covenant), then God could justly be charged with breaking his promises, for not all of them are saved. But Wilson, wanting to "recover the objectivity of the covenant," that is, wanting to understand the Covenant as the unbelieving Jews misunderstood it, denies the relevance of the doctrine of election to this matter – he denigrates election as a "secret thing" that belongs only to God (how foolish of God, then, to reveal the doctrine to men) – and asserts that all the baptized are "members of the covenant" and recipients of the promises of life and salvation. But if God made no promise of life and salvation to all the circumcised, and if circumcision is the analogue of ritual baptism, then God today makes no promise of life and salvation to all the baptized.

How does Wilson try to exculpate God from the charge of breaking his alleged promises of life and salvation to those who are baptized? Like the Arminians and Roman Catholics, Wilson makes the promises of life and salvation depend on man's response to the offer of salvation: God makes conditional promises of life and salvation to all the baptized (and circumcised), and they, in turn, must meet the conditions of salvation in order to obtain final salvation. If they perform satisfactorily, they are blessed with eternal life and salvation. If they fail to perform satisfactorily, they are cursed with eternal death and damnation. Their destiny depends on their meeting the conditions of the covenant – not on the work of a Representative or Substitute, for Christ the Mediator plays little or no role in Wilson's doctrine of the objective covenant and salvation. In Wilson's theology, God helps those who help themselves.

Wilson substitutes his objective covenant for the Covenant of Grace, and the sinner must personally meet the conditions of Wilson's covenant (through his "covenantal faithfulness") in order to receive the benefits and blessings of Wilson's covenant. That is, Wilson teaches legalism – salvation by obedience and works – under the guise of covenant. In this Wilson is not alone. David Engelsma of the Protestant Reformed Seminary writes:

> The significant contemporary development of covenant doctrine...concerns the issue whether the covenant of God with His people in Jesus Christ is unconditional or conditional. The new teaching that troubles the Reformed churches, and threatens to carry them away, is the natural, indeed inevitable, development of the doctrine that the covenant [of Grace] is conditional. It is necessary, therefore, that we have the issue of the conditionality or unconditionality of the covenant clearly in mind. In considering the controversy, we must remember that the covenant of God with His people is central to the revelation of God in Scripture and to the redemption that is at the heart of biblical revelation....
>
> That the covenant [of Grace] is unconditional means that the establishing, maintaining, and perfecting of that blessed relationship of love and communion between God and a man do not depend on the sinful man; that the blessings which the covenant brings to the man do not depend upon him; and that the final, everlasting salvation enjoyed by one with whom God makes His covenant does not depend upon that man. There is no work of the sinner that is a condition he must fulfill in order to have the covenant, or to enjoy its blessings.
>
> Unconditionality rules out merit, or earning. It also

> rules out all effort by the sinner, even though not meritorious, upon which the covenant and its blessings are supposed to depend, or which cooperates with God in establishing and maintaining the covenant and in bestowing the benefits of the covenant.... We do not earn, and thus deserve, the covenant [of Grace]. But unconditionality also rules out all works that distinguish one man from another, or that are the reason why the covenant is given to one and not to another, or that obtain the covenant, which God merely makes available.... The reason why all such works are excluded, along with meritorious works, is that these works, as much as meritorious works, would make the sinner his own savior and rob God of the glory of salvation.
>
> Such is the development of the doctrine of a conditional covenant in our day that it overthrows the entire theological system of salvation by sovereign grace as confessed by the Reformed faith in the Canons of Dordt and in the Westminster Standards. The doctrine of a conditional covenant is explained by its advocates [in a way that denies] the heart of the Gospel of grace, namely, justification by faith alone on the basis only of the lifelong obedience and atoning death of Jesus Christ.[31]

Consider again these verses, as well as the passages from the Westminster Standards quoted above, to see how different Wilson's objective covenant is from the Covenant of Grace:

> Behold, the days are coming, says the Lord, when I will make a new covenant with the house of Israel and with the house of Judah – not according to the covenant that I made with their fathers in the day that I took them

31. Editorial, *The Standard Bearer*, January 1, 2003. In the mid-twentieth century Klaas Schilder preached the doctrine of a conditional covenant in the Netherlands and contributed to the apostasy of the Reformed churches there.

> by the hand to bring them out of the land of Egypt, my covenant which they broke, though I was a husband to them, says the Lord. But this is the covenant that I will make with the house of Israel after those days, says the Lord: I will put my law in their minds, and write it on their hearts; and I will be their God, and they shall be my people.... No more shall every man teach his neighbor, and every man his brother, saying "Know the Lord," for they all shall know me, from the least of them to the greatest of them, says the Lord. For I will forgive their iniquity, and their sin I will remember no more [*Jeremiah* 31:31-34].

In the Covenant of Grace, God promises salvation to all members of the Covenant, and God keeps his promises: He actually gives salvation to all members of his Covenant. Not one person for whom Christ died is lost. Not one member of the Covenant of Grace goes to Hell. God does not break any promise of salvation to those who are outside the Covenant of Grace, for he makes no promise of salvation to anyone outside the Covenant of Grace. Effectual calling, regeneration, justification, belief of the Gospel, adoption, sanctification, perseverance, and glorification are not conditions for establishing or maintaining the Covenant of Grace; they are in fact the benefits, the blessings of the Covenant, which God gives freely, unilaterally, and unconditionally to all those he has chosen to save by Christ. By his obedience to the Father, Christ obtained all these blessings for his people, and he gives them freely and infallibly to them. Unlike Wilson's objective covenant, the Covenant of Grace is an efficacious covenant: "And I will make an everlasting covenant with them, that I will not turn away from doing them good; but I will put my fear in their hearts so that they will not depart from me" (*Jeremiah* 32:40). God unilaterally made this Covenant of Grace; God alone maintains it in force; and it is an everlasting and efficacious Covenant. God puts his Spirit into the hearts of his chosen people so that they *cannot* depart from him. "I will give you a new heart and put a new spirit within you; I will take the heart of stone out of your flesh and give you a heart of flesh. I will put my Spirit within you and cause you to walk in my statutes, and you will keep my judgments and do them" (*Ezekiel* 36:26-27). When God speaks in the future tense – "I will give, I will take, I will put, you will keep" – those events must happen. *They cannot not happen*. Even the good works of his people are guaranteed by the efficacious Covenant of Grace. God changes our hearts; he puts his Spirit within us; and he causes us to walk in his statutes. Paul echoes *Ezekiel* in his letter to the Ephesians:

> Blessed be the God and Father of our Lord Jesus Christ, who has blessed us with every spiritual blessing in the heavenly places in Christ, just as he chose us in him before the foundation of the world, that we should be holy and without blame before him in love, having predestined us to adoption as sons by Jesus Christ to himself, according to the good pleasure of his will, to the praise of the glory of his grace, by which he has made us accepted in the beloved. In him we have redemption through his blood, the forgiveness of sins, according to the riches of his grace, which he made to abound toward us in all wisdom and prudence.... For by grace you have been saved through faith, and that not of yourselves; it is the gift of God, not of works, lest anyone should boast. For we are his workmanship, created in Christ Jesus for good works, which God prepared beforehand that we should walk in them [*Ephesians* 1:3-8; 2:8-10].

So far are individual election and predestination from being at odds with the Covenant of Grace that one cannot understand the Covenant of Grace, its promises, and its efficacy apart from those doctrines. That is why Paul explains the Covenant of Grace in *Romans* 9 by the doctrine of individual election. One can understand the Covenant of Grace only if one understands God's eternal election of individuals. Election and predestination are doctrines of grace that inform the Covenant of Grace. By eliminating the doctrine of individual election from his covenant – so as to make it objective – Wilson invents a different covenant.

Here is a simple chart comparing Wilson's objective covenant with the Covenant of Grace:

	Wilson's Covenant	*Covenant of Grace*
Who are the parties?	God and all baptized/ circumcised persons	God the Father and the Lord Jesus Christ
Who are the members?	All baptized/ circumcised persons	Elect individuals
What are the conditions members must meet for receiving salvation?	Covenantal faithfulness	None
Who meets the conditions of salvation?	Members keep or break the covenant	Jesus Christ, as the Mediator, the Representative of and Substitute for his people, meets the conditions of the Covenant of Works
How is one saved?	Initial grace conferred by ritual baptism, plus good works	Christ's righteousness imputed through belief alone
Outcome of the covenant	Depends on the sinner's performance	Depends on Christ alone, who guarantees salvation for all members

9. The New Birth

Wilson either does not understand or wants to redefine the term "new birth" as well. He writes, "And Jesus does not limit this [being born again] to individual men – *all Israel* must be born again (*John* 3:7), which is what happened at Pentecost" (34-35).

What is a rational person to make of statements such as this? Is Wilson suggesting that no one in that upper room, including the apostles, was born again before Pentecost? It would seem so, for any other meaning would indicate that he is equivocating on the phrase "born again." Is he suggesting that the Holy Spirit's giving of the gift of speaking foreign languages without having studied them is the same as being born again? If so, where is the argument from Scripture that supports this peculiar notion? Is he suggesting that because there was a visible, presumably photographable, representation of the Holy Spirit at Pentecost that this is somehow the real thing, and God's changing of individual minds is subjective and "ethereal"? Or is he suggesting that because Pentecost involves a lot of individuals receiving the gift of the Spirit at the same time that this is "all Israel" being "born again"? Whatever Wilson means, there is no Scriptural support for it, and so he offers none. He merely asserts.

Here is what Jesus told Nicodemus in *John* 3:7: "Do not marvel that I said to you, 'You must be born again.'" That's it. Contrary to Wilson, the verse does not say "all Israel" must be born again; still less that this is what happened at Pentecost. Neither Israel nor Pentecost is even mentioned in the single verse Wilson cites. Wilson must hold his readers in utter contempt, thinking they are either too stupid or too cowardly to question him on such false assertions.

But let us suppose the verse did say what Wilson imagines it to say. The contrast Wilson imagines – between "all Israel" and "individual men" – simply is not there: Only individual men can be born again, born from above, in the proper meaning of the phrase, because *only individual men are souls.* There is no collective soul. The fact that Christ used a plural pronoun in *John* 3:7 does not make the verse refer to anything other than individual souls. Christ meant that everyone, including Nicodemus, the teacher of the Jews, must be born again by the Spirit in order to see and to enter the kingdom of Heaven.[32]

Christ's emphasis on the salvation of the individual throughout his conversation with Nicodemus is hard to miss, given all the singular pronouns, nouns, and verbs he uses: "Except *a man*...*he* cannot see.... Except *a man*... *he* cannot enter.... So *is every one who is* born of the Spirit.... *Whosoever believes*.... *He* that *believes* on him.... *He* that *believes* not....*he has* not believed.... *Every one* that *does* evil... *his* deeds.... *He* that *does* truth.... *his* deeds...." There is absolutely nothing in the passage that would suggest that something other than a person – an individual soul – could or must be born again. But Wilson's disdain for both the individual and the invisible makes him miss what Christ says. According to Wilson, religious emphasis on individuals is caused by "rationalism" and "modernism." That makes Christ a rationalist and a modernist, for Christ emphasized the salvation of the individual throughout his ministry.

Wilson is manically emphatic: "*the new birth is a reality*" (35), he says, thumping the table. Well, so is streptococcus. So what? What we want and need to know is, What does Wilson mean when he uses the term "new birth"? Obviously his new

32. Christ was telling Nicodemus that his godly heritage was not sufficient for salvation; his circumcision, his descent from Abraham, his covenant faithfulness fell far short of the requirements of the kingdom.

theology, in which basic terms such as "Christianity" and "covenant" are redefined, requires him also to redefine "new birth." It is meaningless and useless to say – no matter how many italics and bold-faced letters one uses – that something is a "reality." Everything is a "reality." We want to know *what* Wilson thinks the new birth is. And once again Wilson fails us. Nicodemus found Jesus' words hard to believe because he misunderstood them as referring to a visible birth; but at least Nicodemus correctly understood that Jesus' words apply to individuals rather than to collectives. Nicodemus did not understand that the new birth is *invisible*, which is why Jesus used the illustration of the wind and mentioned the work of the Holy Spirit. Had Jesus meant "corporate regeneration" (whatever that means), as Wilson bizarrely asserts of *John* 3:7, Jesus could have said that very clearly to Nicodemus. But Jesus did not mean "corporate regeneration," so he did not say it. He spoke only of the Holy Spirit sovereignly and invisibly regenerating those individuals chosen for eternal life.

10. The Arch-Heresy of Individualism

Wilson devotes an entire chapter to attacking individualism.[33] He first tries to mislead the reader with a culinary metaphor: "There is no tension between omelettes and eggs" (57). In Wilson's analogy, eggs represent individuals and omelettes represent the whole, what he calls "a corporate covenant omelette." This is a strange metaphor for a professed Christian to use, since it was made notorious by the first Soviet dictator Vladimir Lenin: "One cannot make omelettes without breaking eggs." In saying this, Lenin was defending his bloody Com-

33. Wilson's antipathy toward individuals and individualism permeates his book. Chapter 16 on "Heretics and the Covenant" opens by calling individualism an "arch-heresy."

munist Revolution. But Lenin, more perceptive than Wilson, understood that there is indeed a "tension" between omelettes and eggs, because eggs must be broken and scrambled in order to make an omelette. Like Wilson, Lenin was a collectivist – Wilson in a theological and ecclesiastical sense, and Lenin in an economic and political sense; but unlike Wilson, Lenin did not pretend that there is no tension between omelettes and eggs. In Wilson's theology and in Lenin's political philosophy, eggs – individuals – must be broken and their individuality destroyed in order to make the collective omelette.

Now the Bible denies that God makes saved individuals into collective omelettes. (Perhaps the damned are broken and scrambled, but the elect are not.) Instead of teaching that individuals and individuality gradually disappear into a "corporate covenant omelette," the Bible asserts a crescendo of individuality, until finally, in the eternal state, the individual has a direct and private relationship with Christ that no one else shares: "To him who overcomes I will give some of the hidden manna to eat. And I will give him a white stone, and on the stone a new name written which no one knows except him who receives it" (*Revelation* 2:17). The Bible, from its beginning in *Genesis* with the creation of the individual Adam (who was before all and is the source of all the families and nations of the Earth), to its end in *Revelation* (there are no families in Heaven[34] but only individuals who have a private relationship to Christ), teaches the value and primacy of the individual soul. Wilson's attack on individuals and individualism in the name of medieval collectivism is a repudiation of the Bible's teaching.

Through the centuries foolish theologians have connected

34. Those who exaggerate the importance of family may be offended at what Christ said: "For in the resurrection they neither marry nor are given in marriage, but are like angels of God in Heaven" (*Matthew* 22:30). Perhaps Mormonism, with its doctrine of eternal marriage, is closer to their theology of the family.

individuality with sinfulness, and the disappearance of sinfulness, according to them, requires the disappearance of individuality. Their hellish vision is one in which all individuals are broken and scrambled into one Grand Omelette. Wilson's metaphor is the metaphor the Communists used, not the metaphor Scripture uses. The Scriptural metaphor is not an omelette, but a human body, in which each part – the eye, the ear, the hand – retains and glories in its individuality, while contributing to the well-being of the whole. In the Scriptural metaphor – but not in Wilson's and Lenin's collectivist metaphor – the eye becomes more discerning, the ear more acute, the hand more dexterous, by being joined to the Head. The intensification and enhancement of their individuality benefits both them and the whole body. They are not scrambled into some homogeneous omelette in which there is neither eye nor hand nor ear nor head. They become better in their individual purposes and functions, and because they become better individuals, they benefit the body more and more.

Wilson seems to remember, dimly, that the Bible says something about the value and importance of the individual. After his initial attack on the individual, he starts to retreat. He defines "individualism" as "the deification of self" (58). Now who, one must ask, outside Max Stirner, whom Wilson has probably never heard of, Friedrich Nietzsche, or Ayn Rand – none of whom Wilson mentions, of course – ever suggested such a thing? Wilson's purpose in offering such a definition is clear: He resumes his assault on his opponents in the churches, now charging them with advocating individualism, that is, the "deification of self." He never condescends to cite even one sentence from anyone saying any such thing. Supplying evidence for his assertions is beneath him. Wilson smears by imputing his peculiar definition of individualism to all advocates of individualism and accusing them of sin.

Wilson's theological collectivism is thoroughgoing. He asserts: "We are what we are because of covenant relations" (58). According to Wilson, covenant is primary, not persons. But *Genesis* disagrees: Adam the individual was what he was because of the decree and creative activity of God, not because of "covenant relations." God made no covenant with Adam until after Adam had been created. Adam was the image of God before God made a covenant with him. (And Wilson, ironically, denies this Covenant of Works.) And every individual soul is what he is for the same reason: the invisible decree of God. *Genesis* says the individual came first, and then later the family, the church, business, society, and civil government, all derivative from that individual. Today a person is born into a family, but that family itself was created by the informed consent of two individuals, whose consent makes it a family.[35]

"A man," Wilson pontificates, "is not defined by his internal essence" (58). On the contrary, that is precisely what a man is "defined by." A man is the image of God; he is the breath of God, rationality. Wilson continues his attack on the individual: "Everyone is someone's daughter or someone's son" (59). This is desipience. Those relationships may make that person a daughter or a son; they do not make that person a person. He or she must be a person before he or she can be a son or a daughter. The concept son and the concept daughter logically depend on the concept person, individual. Is Wilson here trying to assert some sophomoric version of Hegelian metaphysics? Who knows? But the purpose of all this nonsense seems clear: It is to assert – just as Hegel did,

35. Wilson and Wilkins superstitiously think that rituals make marriages. In the *Genesis* account of Adam and Eve, there is no ritual, merely consent. It is the informed, rational consent of the parties that makes a marriage, not some ritual performed by a priest.

and especially his totalitarian disciples Marx and Lenin – the primacy of the collective.

There is so much about the importance of the individual in Scripture that Wilson cannot ignore it. He does his best to twist it to his own purposes. Consider this sentence: "A man who loves his individual soul will pursue wisdom, which cannot be pursued outside the corporate covenant boundaries of the Church" (59). Loves his individual soul? *Mirabile dictu*, this sounds like individualism – and indeed it is, sanctioned by *Proverbs* and the rest of Scripture. Wilson cannot deny that that is what Scripture says. So he must do his best to misinterpret it, and here we have a clue to Wilson's whole enterprise: He intends to make the institutional church a substitute for Christ, the visible for the invisible, the earthly for the heavenly. This is good medieval ecclesiology, but it is not Christian theology. Furthermore, Wilson furnishes no reason – and there is no Biblical reason – for his assertion that one cannot pursue wisdom outside the boundaries of the institutional church. *Non sapientia ex ecclesia* is not a Biblical idea. The Biblical idea is *non sapientia ex Scriptura* – but that leaves those annoying individuals without proper supervision, and no good collectivist can tolerate that.

11. Justification Not by Faith Alone

Now that Wilson has redefined "Christian," "church," "covenant," and "new birth," he is ready to redefine justification as well. He writes, "We are saved by grace through faith, which is not the same thing as *faithlessly* clutching a proposition that we are saved by grace through faith" (42). After noting that Wilson omits the word *alone* from his formulation, and thus differs from the Reformers and agrees with the Romanists, we wonder, what does the phrase "clutching a proposition" mean?

How does one clutch something invisible and intangible? Could Wilson mean "believing a proposition"? But he wrote "faithlessly," so he cannot mean "believing." So how exactly does one "clutch a proposition faithlessly"? We have no idea, and neither does Wilson. He uses the phrase for its dramatic effect; it has no intelligible meaning.

This is Wilson's first mention of propositions, and he makes it clear that he dislikes them, perhaps even more than he dislikes individuals and things invisible. This is too bad, for Christianity consists of propositions: There are thousands of them in the Word of God, all revealed by God for our learning, belief, salvation, growth in knowledge, and edification in the truth. Wilson's hostility to propositions and knowledge is his hostility to Christianity. His employee and fellow medievalist Peter Leithart makes that hostility to Christianity clear in his book, *Against Christianity*:

> The Bible never mentions Christianity. It does not preach Christianity, nor does it encourage us to preach Christianity. Paul did not preach Christianity, nor did any of the other apostles. During the centuries when the Church was strong and vibrant, she did not preach Christianity either. Christianity, like Judaism and "Yahwism," is an invention of biblical scholars, theologians, and politicians, and one of its chief effects is to keep Christians and the Church in their proper marginal place. The Bible speaks of Christians and of the Church, but Christianity is gnostic, and the Church firmly rejected gnosticism from her earliest days. Christianity is the heresy of heresies....[36]

And so the Antichristian drivel continues.

36. Peter Leithart, *Against Christianity*. Moscow, Idaho: Canon Press, 2003, 13.

Just a page later, Wilson refers to "law and gospel divisions or grace and works divisions" as "a trap." In saying this, Wilson is rejecting the Reformation and Reformed theology, with its contrast between Law and Gospel, works and faith. That contrast is clearly stated in Scripture: "Did you receive the Spirit by the works of the law, *or* by the hearing of faith?" (*Galatians* 3:2). In this verse the Apostle Paul acknowledges and asserts an either-or, an antithesis, not a synthesis, between works of the law and the hearing of faith. The Holy Spirit and the apostle say (1) it cannot be both works of the law and faith; (2) it must be one or the other; (3) there is no third possibility; and (4) the two are not the same. Paul's rhetorical question requires a specific answer: "We received the Spirit by the hearing of faith alone." This is consistent with what Paul wrote elsewhere: "Now to him who works, the wages are not counted as grace but as debt. But to him *who does not work but believes* on him who justifies the ungodly, his belief is accounted for righteousness" (*Romans* 4:4-5). In these verses Paul asserts an antithesis between works and grace, Law and Gospel. It is "him who does not work, but believes," that is justified. Wilson says this is a "trap." Is the Holy Spirit laying a trap for us? Or is Douglas Wilson?

Wilson defends the Apostles' Creed's silence on saving faith: "It [the Creed] is not [deficient], precisely because the early Christians were *confessing* their faith, not talking about it" (41).[37] This is a textbook example of equivocation. Indeed, one could use Wilson's whole book as a source of examples of logical fallacies when teaching logic. The so-called Apostles' Creed is

37. The name of the so-called Apostles' Creed is a hoax. The Creed was not written, approved, or recited by the apostles. Its name is misleading, for it was used for political purposes. Like the fraudulent *Donation of Constantine*, the Apostles' Creed was used to solidify the control of the Roman Church-State over churches in the West. The Creed omits the *sine qua non* of Christianity: justification by faith alone, not even mentioning the substitutionary atonement of Christ.

silent on "faith," understood in the sense of "the mental activity of believing," which is what unites sinners to Christ. The Creed says nothing about faith in that sense, though Scripture says a great deal about it. This is a serious defect in the Apostles' Creed, and one more reason that it should not be recited in Christian churches.[38] But in his rejoinder, Wilson equivocates on the term "faith" and uses the word "faith" in the sense of "doctrines believed" : "They were confessing their faith." Perhaps Wilson fails to understand the difference between the two senses of the word "faith." Perhaps he doesn't even realize he is equivocating. Perhaps he does, and he says it anyway.

Wilson then manages to slur both the *solas* of the Reformation and those who defend them as unbelievers: "merit-mongering is not the only mongering possible. There is also the problem of *sola*-mongering. This error is committed when faith is honored and talked about endlessly – but not exercised" (43). He expands on this smear: "The other [enemy] is inside the camp and professes itself to be a friend. The controversy that swirls around the objectivity of the covenant exists in part because there are some who want *solas* they hold in their hand – which keeps those *solas* out of the heart and life and family" (44). So Wilson accuses some of his opponents – unnamed, of course – of being unbelievers. His critics do not exercise Christian faith. They are enemies inside the camp. They profess to be friends. They do not have the *solas* in their hearts. *Mirabile dictu*, Wilson can see the invisible after all.

Wilson continues his attack on propositions: "I do not deny the propositional truth the *solas* refer to, but [you knew that *but* was coming, didn't you?] I do maintain that to limit them to mere propositions is to kill them. Faith without works is

38. For an excellent analysis of the Creed, see Cliffton R. Loucks, "Rethinking the Apostles' Creed," *The Trinity Review*, March/April 2003. The essay is available at http://www.trinityfoundation.org/ in the Review Archives.

dead. The five *solas* without works are dead too. Propositions without works are dead – even if the propositions are true."

This anti-intellectual, irrational outburst reveals the root of Wilson's heresy. He says, contradicting Christ, true propositions are dead, apart from works. Christ said,

> The words that I speak to you are Spirit, and they are life [*John* 6:63].
>
> Most assuredly I say to you, he who hears my word and believes in him who sent me has [right now, not after doing some good works] everlasting life, and shall not come into judgment, but has [already] passed from death to life [*John* 5:24].

It is merely by hearing and believing, as Paul says, not by doing the works of the law, that one is saved. James, whom Wilson quotes but does not understand, himself speaks of "the implanted word which is able to save your souls" (1:21). It is the word, the propositions of the Gospel, the doctrine, the theology, apart from works, that saves souls. Truth is not dead; it is living and life-giving. James further declares, "Of his own will he [God] brought us forth by the word of truth, that we might be a kind of first-fruits of his creatures" (1:18). It is the word of truth, the propositions of the Gospel, that regenerates us. It is not works that we have done that bring life and salvation. Salvation is by faith-apart-from-works, not by faith-with-works. "It [my word] shall not return to me void," God says, "but it shall accomplish what I please, and it shall prosper in the thing for which I sent it" (*Isaiah* 55:11). "Your word has given me life," says the psalmist (*Psalm* 119:50). "You have the words of eternal life," says Peter (*John* 6:68). "...holding fast the word of life" (*Philippians* 2:16).

Contrary to Wilson's Antichristian attack on words, the Gospel propositions are alive, and they give eternal life to those elected and appointed to life.[39] They are not dead, and they do not require our working in order to become alive. In fact, Wilson has things backwards: It is the true words, the propositions, that bring forth good works, not the works that make propositions living. The propositions are living and the source of life, and works are a kind of fruit of that life – a result, an effect of the living propositions. Wilson pontificates, "understanding these prepositions" – presumably he means "propositions," though his tirade against propositions makes one wonder – must be "in the gut." Because his intellectual life is invisible, Wilson belittles thinking and propositions, and speaks of understanding "in the gut" – which is quite visible. Wilson espouses an excerebrose, intestinal religion.

Wilson asserts that "*individual* justification...occurs at the moment an unconverted man is converted from darkness to light" (47). His wording here is ambiguous and misleading, for justification is not something that occurs within the man, but God's legal pronouncement that he is righteous. Wilson seems to be confusing justification and conversion, but his words are so ambiguous they could be read another way. Wilson distinguishes this individual justification from "corporate justification, which...does not contradict the realities of individual justification. Rather it places those individual realities in a justified context," whatever that means (47). This statement seems to make both individual and corporate justification subjective changes in the sinner and the church. Wilson teaches what he calls "corporate regeneration" and "corporate Christianity." This is equivocation cubed, for what he means by "corporate" is not the whole body of believers, that is, justified or regenerate persons; but a collective that includes

39. See *Mark* 8:38: "For whoever is ashamed of me and my words in this adulterous and sinful generation, of him the Son of Man also will be ashamed when he comes in the glory of his Father with the holy angels."

those who are unregenerate, unjustified, unbelieving, and even reprobate. In Wilson's Wonderland, the reprobate are elect, the unjustified are justified, and the unregenerate are saved. Wilson equivocates on "regenerate" and "justified," for when he applies those terms to a promiscuous group, they cannot mean what they mean when applied to elect individuals. A regenerate individual is one made alive by the action of the Holy Spirit in his mind. A group has no mind, and a promiscuous group of believers and unbelievers is never made alive by the Holy Spirit. A justified soul is one declared righteous by God, and the righteousness of Christ is imputed to his account. A group has no soul, and a promiscuous group is never the recipient of Christ's imputed righteousness. But Wilson's medieval corporatism requires him to make individual justification depend on "corporate justification." Of course, he cites no Scripture to support this theological fiction.

Of justification Wilson writes,

> The Bible says that baptism saves. Why do we not use this language? It is because our systematic language has replaced scriptural language. And although I hold to *sola fide* as the right scriptural interpretation, I have to do so recognizing that the only time the Bible uses the phrase "faith alone," it does so in order to deny it. "Ye see then how that by works a man is justified, and not by faith only" (Jas. 2:24).

Wilson, of course, is echoing Roman Catholic apologists such as Robert Sungenis when he says that the only time the Bible uses the phrase "faith alone" it does so in order to deny it.[40] To use another Latin phrase, this issue is a *pons asinorum*.

40. Wilson includes a chapter (21) near the end of the book titled "The Greatness of Justification by Faith." The word "alone" is missing from both the chapter title and chapter. A typical sentence is, "To be justified is to be declared righteous, and of course we are justified through faith in believing God's declarations" (178). No informed Romanist would disagree.

The Bible never uses the word "Trinity" or the phrase "covenant of works." Do we then conclude that they are not taught in Scripture? By what argument? The Scriptures repeatedly use the phrase "free will" and use it favorably. Do we conclude from this fact that the Bible teaches free will? By what argument? Or do we read Scripture intelligently, rather than stupidly? Wilson's point is very simple: We ought to say "baptism saves," as well as whatever conflicting expressions we wish. Scripture is paradoxical, and "we cannot let our systematic language replace it."

Wilson doesn't understand *Titus* 3:5, which is a verse he cites to support his view that baptism saves. He writes:

> Another obvious means of grace is baptism – we were saved, not by our own works, but by the washing of regeneration and renewal by the Holy Spirit (*Titus* 3:4-6). The result of this is that we are justified by His grace (v. 7). The Lord's Supper is another important means – we are to be established by eating grace, not Jewish sacrifices (Heb. 13:9).

Wilson is such a materialist that he thinks grace can be eaten.[41]

Nor does Wilson understand *1 Peter* 3:18-22. He writes: "Water baptism now saves us. Peter tells us that baptism saves..." (100). These words appear 14 lines after Wilson quoted the passage from Peter, in which Peter denies that water baptism saves us: "The like figure whereunto even baptism does also now save us (not the putting away of the filth of the flesh, but the answer of a good conscience toward God) by the resurrection of Jesus Christ." Apparently every time Wilson sees the word "baptism" in the text, he thinks of ritual, water baptism. After all, water is visible, and baptism by the Spirit, as well as the conscience, is invisible.

41. For an explanation of *Titus* 3:4-6 that does not deny justification by faith alone, see Gordon H. Clark, *The Pastoral Epistles*. The Trinity Foundation, 1999.

Wilson brazenly asserts that the *Westminster Confession* teaches baptismal regeneration: "the Westminster Confession taught baptismal regeneration" (103). He quotes 28.1, which says no such thing. Wilson even asserts his own version of apostolic succession: "There is an apostolic succession in the Church, but it is not a succession delivered through ordination. Rather, it is a succession of baptisms..." (107). But since Wilson's rite of baptism must be performed by "an authorized representative of the Christian church," how much different is Wilson's apostolic succession from Rome's? To have a succession of legitimate baptisms, one must also have a succession of legitimate authorizations, that is, ordinations. Neither Wilson nor Rome understands that the "successors" of the apostles are the writings of the apostles, that is, the Scriptures. They and only they speak with divine and apostolic authority.

Part of the explanation for Wilson's heterodox view of the sacraments (his view of the Supper is as non-Biblical as his view of baptism) is that he insists that "grace is mediated" (110). He denies that God acts immediately on the soul, but always acts through visible or at least sensate means: water, wine, bread. He contradicts the words of Christ: "Flesh and blood has not revealed this to you, but my Father who is in Heaven" (*Matthew* 16:17). Wilson and his accomplices want to deny the direct and immediate action of the Holy Spirit on the minds of men, because such action does not allow the institutional church to be the indispensable dispenser of grace. Their purpose is to maximize the role of the institutional church and to minimize the role of the Holy Spirit in saving men. That is why he writes scornfully and blasphemously of "refried gnosticism" and "invisible conduits" between the Spirit and the believer.

In addition to teaching that (1) ritual baptism saves men and (2) that there is a baptismal succession, Wilson teaches the real presence of Christ in the Supper. He writes: "*The Westminster Confession teaches that there is a real presence of Christ's body and blood in the act of faithful eating at His Table*" (111 – emphasis is Wilson's). Of course the *Confession* teaches no such thing, and Wilson does not quote it saying any such thing. He writes, "Christ is presented to us in the sacrament. We see Him there by *faith*, not by sight."[42] Rome, of course, says the same thing. Rome denies that sight sees Christ, but asserts his real, that is, physical presence nonetheless. Wilson's insistence on the "real presence of Christ's body and blood," unaccompanied by the *Confession's* repeated statements that Christ is not "carnally and corporally present" at the Supper, is similar to Rome's view of the real presence. Especially so since Wilson has already emphatically told us that the objective is the visible and sensate, and that "seeing by faith" is not seeing at all.

12. The Biblical Covenant of Grace

The New Testament is a fuller, clearer, and more systematic revelation of Jesus Christ than the Old. The New Covenant is superior to the Old, as the author of the book of *Hebrews* argues at length, and the revelation of the New Covenant is superior to the Old. Both are, of course, the Word of God, but "in these last days [God] has spoken to us by his Son [not merely by the prophets], who [is] the brightness of his glory and the express image of his person."

Not only does the New Testament give us a fuller, clearer, and more systematic revelation of Jesus Christ than the Old, it also is the authoritative interpretation of the Old. It does this in four ways: (1) by commenting explicitly upon the text of the

42. This is an odd statement from a man who insists that things must be visible in order to be objective.

Old Testament; (2) by incorporating Old Testament texts into its own arguments; (3) by repealing portions of the Mosaic system that are obsolete; and (4) by correcting the common misinterpretations of the Old Testament taught by the Jewish religious leaders of the first century – what some recent theologians call "Second Temple Judaism." Perhaps the most obvious example of the last is Christ's Sermon on the Mount, in which he corrects the false teaching of the rabbis in this way: "You have heard it said....but I say unto you." There are many examples of the first three methods – commentary on and incorporation of the text of the Old Testament itself, and repeal of its national and sacrificial system – and the one that we shall look at most closely is Paul's letter to the Romans. In this letter, the Apostle Paul is the inspired and authoritative interpreter of the Covenant of Grace; any interpretation of the Covenant that conflicts with the authoritative interpretation written by the Holy Spirit and Paul, either by appealing to the teachings of Second Temple Judaism, or by imposing its own construction on the text of the Old Testament, is false.

Now, what does Paul teach about the Covenant of Grace in *Romans*? First, Paul denies that there is any corporate salvation, any offer of corporate salvation, or corporate election to salvation, as the unbelieving Jews of that day commonly thought. They were falsely assured of their favor with God and of their salvation because they were children of Abraham, in solidarity with the patriarch with whom God had made the covenant. But Paul denounces that assurance in *Romans* 2 and declares the Jews more guilty before God than the Gentiles:

> Indeed you are called a Jew, and rest on the law, and make your boast in God, and know his will, and approve the things that are excellent, being instructed out of the law, and are confident that you yourself are a guide to the blind, a light to those who are in darkness, an in-

> structor of the foolish, a teacher of babes, having the form of knowledge and truth in the law. You, therefore, who teach another, do you not teach yourself? You who preach that a man should not steal, do you steal? You who say, "Do not commit adultery," do you commit adultery? You who abhor idols, do you rob temples? You who make your boast in the law, do you dishonor God through breaking the law? For "the name of God is blasphemed among the Gentiles because of you," as it is written.
>
> For circumcision is indeed profitable if you keep the law; but if you are a breaker of the law, your circumcision has become uncircumcision.... For he is not a Jew who is one outwardly, nor is circumcision that which is outward in the flesh; but he is a Jew who is one inwardly; and circumcision is that of the heart, in the Spirit, not in the letter; whose praise is not from men but from God [*Romans* 2:17-29].

Paul here denies that there is any group justification, corporate election to salvation, or corporate salvation. Rather than assuring their salvation, their outward advantages – chiefly the oracles of God, the Scriptures – condemned the Jews more severely than the Gentiles, who did not have any special revelation from God. Paul concludes his argument with these words: "Now we know that whatever the law says, it says to those who are under the law, that every mouth may be stopped, and all the world may become guilty before God. Therefore by the deeds of the law no flesh will be justified in his sight, for by the law is the knowledge of sin" (*Romans* 3:19-20).

The next step in Paul's argument is to assert not only justification by belief alone, but to insist that justification is taught in the Old Testament: "But now the righteousness of God apart from the law is revealed, being witnessed by *The Law and the Prophets*" (*Romans* 3:21). Paul explicitly attacks the Jewish notion that righteousness comes by the law, and insists that nothing of the sort is taught in *The Law and the Prophets*; in fact, *The Law and the Prophets* teaches that righteousness comes "apart from the law." Furthermore, Paul attacked the Jewish misunderstanding of the covenant by denying that God was the God of all loyal, circumcised Jews because he had entered into covenant with Abraham: "Or is he the God of the Jews only? Is he not also the God of the Gentiles? Yes, of the Gentiles also, since there is one God who will justify the circumcised by faith and the uncircumcised through faith" (*Romans* 3:29-30).

Notice Paul's reason for saying that God is the God of the Gentiles as well as the Jews: justification by faith alone. It was not circumcision, nor Torah, nor descent from Abraham that guaranteed the fulfillment of the promise "I will be their God, and they shall be my people." Today, it is not baptism, nor church membership, nor godly heritage, nor covenant faithfulness that guarantees the fulfillment of that promise, but God alone.

So far in this passage, Paul has asserted:

1. that the circumcision of the Jews does not make them pleasing to God;

2. that being the physical children of Abraham and bearing the signs of the covenant are not assurances of favor with God;

3. that there is no group insurance policy that insures a loyal, circumcised child of Abraham election or salvation;

4. that all circumcised Jews are as guilty before God as uncircumcised Gentiles, and more so;

5. that what makes a true Jew is the invisible circumcision of the heart (which Gentiles may have, and some do have), not the visible circumcision of the flesh;

6. that no one, Jew or Gentile, will be justified by the deeds of the law, done at any time in his life;

7. that justification by belief alone is taught in the Old Testament (which he calls *The Law and the Prophets*), and all the Jews should have understood it;

8. that God is God of both Gentiles and Jews, because justification is by belief, not heritage, alone;

9. that belief alone makes God our God, and we his people, thus uniting us to Christ and fulfilling the promise God made to Abraham;

10. that righteousness does not come by the law.

Paul continues his explanation of the Covenant of Grace by focusing on Abraham, whose descendants the Jews were. In *Romans* 4 Paul mentions the doctrine of imputation 11 times – a doctrine that the Jews in general simply did not understand. Abraham was saved by an imputed righteousness, a righteousness not his own. He was saved while he was still uncircumcised. Physical circumcision, to which the Jews looked for assurance of their favor with God, had no part to play in Abraham's salvation – and it has no part to play in the salvation of his children either. "For circumcision is indeed profitable if you keep the law [and no one does], but if you are a breaker of the law [and everyone is] your circumcision has become uncircumcision." Further, "this blessedness" (*Romans* 4:6, 9) that is, salvation apart from works, comes on all who believe, whether they are physically circumcised or not. Paul further explained the reasons:

> For the promise that he would be the heir of the world was not to Abraham or to his seed through the law, but through the righteousness of faith. For if those who are of the law are heirs, faith is made void and the promise made of no effect, because the law brings about wrath; for where there is no law there is no transgression. Therefore it is of faith that it might be according to grace, so

> that the promise might be sure to all the seed, not only to those who are of the law, but also to those who are of the faith of Abraham, who is the father of us all [*Romans* 4:13-16].

The first reason for justification by faith alone that Paul presents is that the promise was not made to Abraham or his seed through the law, that is through their law-keeping, as the Jews misunderstood the Covenant, but through the righteousness received by faith alone. Paul says that if those who are of the law – those who bear the marks of the covenant and keep their noses clean, those whom Calvin called "saintlings" – are heirs of the promise, then the promise is made of no effect, for they are not saved, but objects of wrath. Notice Paul's argument here: The Jewish misinterpretation of the Covenant makes the promise of the Covenant ineffective ("of no effect"), for the circumcised are not saved, but are objects of wrath, just as he had proved in chapter 2. This is the same Jewish misinterpretation of the Covenant that infected medieval churches, Reformed churches in Europe in the eighteenth and nineteenth centuries, and American Presbyterian and Reformed churches in the twentieth and twenty-first centuries. In the place of an effective, efficacious Covenant of Grace, in which God writes his laws in the minds of all the members of the Covenant, these churches substitute an ineffective, objective covenant in which reprobate (children of the flesh) and elect (children of the promise) alike receive the promises of God in baptism. In opposition to this counterfeit covenant, Paul teaches a Covenant of Grace in which "*the promise might be sure to all the seed*." There is no sure promise of salvation in Wilson's counterfeit covenant. His appeal to ritual baptism for assurance is asinine, for he admits that some baptized people go to Hell.

At this point in his argument, the Apostle Paul discusses the role of the Mediator of the Covenant of Grace, who fulfills the law of God perfectly on behalf of and instead of his people, and who dies the death demanded by the law for their sin, paying the full penalty due to them. Because he is the Mediator of the Covenant for his people, their union with Christ, the Covenant Head, results in their receiving the free gift of salvation, freedom from the condemnation of the law (they are "dead to the law through the body of Christ" their substitute), and all the blessings of the Covenant of Grace, including regeneration and faith itself. This is exactly what God had promised in *Jeremiah* 31, as repeated in *Hebrews* 8.

This "new covenant" (not the covenant made with Moses, and explained in greater detail in the New Testament), this Covenant of Grace, is personal ("I will put"; "all shall know me"); individual ("I will put my laws in their minds and write them on their hearts"); and absolutely effective ("I will be their God and they shall be my people;" "None of them shall teach his neighbor...for all shall know me"); and "not according to the covenant that I made with their fathers in the day when I took them by the hand to lead them out of the land of Egypt." The Mosaic covenant was public, corporate, and ineffective ("because they did not continue in my covenant"). By this efficacious, sovereign Covenant of Grace, believers are justified and made sons of God:

> And we know that all things work together for good to those who love God, to those who are the called according to his purpose. For whom he foreknew, he also predestined to be conformed to the image of his Son, that he might be the firstborn among many brethren. Moreover whom he predestined, these he also called; whom he called, these he also justified; and whom he justified, these he also glorified.

> What then shall we say to these things? If God is for us, who can be against us? He who did not spare his own Son, but delivered him up for us all, how shall he not with him also freely give us all things? Who shall bring a charge against God's elect? It is God who justifies. Who is he who condemns? It is Christ who died, and furthermore is also risen, who is even at the right hand of God, who also makes intercession for us. Who shall separate us from the love of Christ? Shall tribulation, or distress, or persecution, or famine, or nakedness, or peril, or sword? As it is written: "For your sake we are killed all day long; we are accounted as sheep for the slaughter."
>
> Yet in all these things we are more than conquerors through him who loved us. For I am persuaded that neither death nor life, nor angels nor principalities nor powers, nor things present nor things to come, nor height nor depth, nor any other created thing, shall be able to separate us from the love of God which is in Christ Jesus our Lord [*Romans* 8:28-39].

This is God's sovereign Covenant of Grace, and it is wholly efficacious; no one and nothing can thwart it. This Covenant is made exclusively with Christ and the elect, to whom alone the promises of life and salvation belong. At this stage in his extended argument, Paul uses the doctrine of election (individual, of course) to defend God against the charge that he has not kept his covenant promises to the Jews, and his Word is of no effect. Paul's argument is, in summary, that God had made no promises of salvation to all the children of Abraham, nor even to all the circumcised, but to his chosen people only. Just as God's election is of some only, and Christ died for some only, so in the Covenant of Grace the promise of salvation is to some only. The Covenant is not a promise to all men, not even to all those that are circumcised or baptized, but only to those chosen by God in Christ from before the foundation of the world. Paul writes: "But it is not that the Word of God has taken no effect. For they are not all Israel who are of Israel, nor are they all children because they are the seed of Abraham; but, "In Isaac your seed shall be called" (*Romans* 9:6-7).

Paul insists that God keeps his promises, that his Word has in fact "taken effect." The problem is not with God's promises, but with those Jews who misunderstand the promises, thinking that God made promises to all the descendants of Abraham, Isaac, and Jacob. To this Paul replies: "They are not all Israel who are of Israel," and "they are not all children of Abraham," echoing his statement in chapter 2: "He is not a Jew who is one outwardly," visibly, but "he is a Jew who is one inwardly," invisibly. Paul quotes the Old Testament making that plain, if only the Jews had believed Moses' writing in *Genesis* 21:12: "In Isaac [not Ishmael] your seed shall be called." But while they trusted in Moses, as Jesus said, they did not understand or believe Moses' words in *Genesis* 21.

Paul continues: "That is, those who are the children of the flesh, these are not the children of God; but the children of the promise are counted as the seed. For this is the word of promise: 'At this time I will come and Sarah shall have a son' " (*Romans* 9:8-9). Paul draws an antithesis between the children of God and the children of the flesh, who are not the children of promise or of God: "These are not the children of God." Those whom the Jews think are the children of God are not. Not only this, but "when Rebecca also had conceived by one man, even by our father Isaac (for the children not yet being born, nor having done any good or evil, that the purpose of God according to election might stand, not of works but of him who calls), it was said to her, 'The older shall serve the younger.' As it is written, 'Jacob I have loved, but Esau I have hated' " (*Romans* 9:10-13).

Paul carries the argument one step further. Not only is the line of circumcised Ishmael not to be identified with the children of God and made recipients of the promises, even though they were children of Abraham and bore the sign of the Covenant, but not all the children of Isaac are children of God either: "Jacob I have loved, but Esau I have hated." The children of God are those whom God has elected, and to them alone are the promises of the Covenant of Grace made.

Paul continues his argument against the unbelieving Jews: "What shall we say then? Is there unrighteousness with God? Certainly not! For he says to Moses, 'I will have mercy on whomever I will have mercy, and I will have compassion on whomever I will have compassion.' So then it is not of him who wills, nor of him who runs, but of God who shows mercy" (*Romans* 9:14-16). The sinner's performance, before or after baptism or circumcision, contributes precisely nothing to his salvation. The Covenant is sovereign; its terms were set unilaterally; and those terms are fulfilled by the God-man who represents his people. The Covenant of Grace accomplishes exactly what God intends. It is to a remnant, not to all Israelites, nor to all church members, that God made his promises:

> Isaiah also cries out concerning Israel: "Though the number of the children of Israel be as the sand of the sea, the remnant will be saved. For he will finish the work and cut it short in righteousness, because the Lord will make a short work upon the Earth." And as Isaiah said before: "Unless the Lord of Sabaoth had left us a seed, we would have become like Sodom, and we would have been made like Gomorrah."
>
> What shall we say then? That Gentiles, who did not pursue righteousness, have attained to righteousness, even the righteousness of faith; but Israel, pursuing the law of righteousness, has not attained to the law of righteous-

> ness. Why? Because they did not seek it by faith, but, as it were, by the works of the law. For they stumbled at that stumbling stone. As it is written: "Behold, I lay in Zion a stumbling stone and rock of offense, and whoever believes on him will not be put to shame" [*Romans* 9:27-33].

Paul explains the Covenant of Grace in terms of God's election of individuals. Any interpretation of the Covenant that excludes or minimizes the doctrine of individual election is a false interpretation. Today ministers in good standing[43] in several denominations, not just Wilson's, are teaching that the Covenant of Grace is conditional, that it is made with all who are baptized, that it is better understood if we ignore the doctrine of election, and that the salvation of the baptized depends upon their fulfilling the terms of the covenant.

To the ten points by which we summarized Paul's teaching earlier, we must now add several more:

11. the sole ground of Abraham's salvation is the imputed righteousness of Christ;

12. this perfect, extrinsic righteousness was imputed to Abraham before he was circumcised; so circumcision (which represents all works done in obedience to God) was neither a condition nor a ground of his salvation, but a result;

13. Christ's righteousness is imputed to believing Jews and Gentiles without partiality;

14. the instrument of this imputation is belief alone, not law-keeping;

15. the Covenant promises of God are not to all the children of Abraham, but only to the children of promise;

43. Some defenders of Neolegalism attack anyone who dares to criticize a "minister in good standing." They cannot understand the elementary point that unless ministers in good standing are criticized, they can never be disciplined. Applied to civil matters, their position is like saying citizens in good standing cannot be accused of crimes. If that were so, no one not already convicted would ever be accused.

16. the Covenant of Grace is made by God the Father with Christ the Mediator, who, acting in the place of (as a substitute for. and on behalf of (as their legal representative), only the people the Father had given him, perfectly fulfills the terms of the Covenant and obtains complete salvation for his people;

17. in the Covenant of Grace God promises all the blessings of the Covenant, including faith and eternal life, to his people;

18. God keeps his Covenant promises by preserving his people for eternity, so that nothing – including they themselves – can separate them from the love of Christ;

19. there is no unrighteousness with God, for he has not broken any promises to his people, but has carried them out fully in Christ.

13. Wilson's Counterfeit Covenant

As we have seen above, Wilson's covenant is not the Covenant of Grace. His rejection of the Covenant of Grace results from the upside-down view he has of all Christianity, in which events – history, not theology – are basic. Like many of our generation, Wilson is still very much a child of the 1960s and 1970s. His arrested development shows not only in his frequent quoting of song lyrics popular during that period, but in the importance he assigns to events – or as they were called back then, "happenings."

Wilson writes: "The subsequent redemptive covenant was equally grounded in history" (64). In this passage Wilson seems to be confusing the Covenant of Redemption with the Covenant of Grace, for the "redemptive covenant" is not subsequent. But he is wrong about both: Neither the Covenant of Redemption nor the Covenant of Grace is "grounded in history." Rather, history is grounded in the invisible and eternal decree of God, and that decree includes the invisible Covenant of Redemption, made between the persons of the Trinity in eternity, and the invisible Covenant of Grace, made between God the Father and the Lord Jesus Christ as the substitute for and representative of his people.[44] To suggest that any divine covenant is "grounded in history" is to get things precisely backwards. Events do not precede thought and doctrine (theology), either logically or chronologically. That is the evolutionary view of the world. The Christian view of the world is that Truth, the Word, Wisdom, Logic is eternal and prior to all history. Christian theology is eternally true, firmly settled, and rigorously systematic; and it precedes all events. It is God's thoughts that produce events. Wilson's error, of course, is not unique to him; it is an error at the heart of the Biblical theology/redemptive history movement, which makes the chronological order in which God revealed truth to men more basic and more important than the logical order the truths themselves possess in God's mind.

Wilson continues: "There is an aspect to such covenants which we may postulate as settled in the mind of God" (64). Now this language – "aspect" and "postulate" – suggests two things: (1) only an "aspect" of the covenant and not the whole covenant may be settled in the mind of God, and (2) we do not know from Scripture that this "aspect" of the covenant is indeed settled in the mind of God; we simply assume it. Neither of Wilson's statements is Scriptural or even compatible with Christianity. Numerous verses of Scripture clearly teach that God knows and plans all of history and redemption, not just an "aspect" of them. Furthermore, these are matters of knowledge revealed in Scripture, and postulations, assumptions, speculations, or hypotheses have nothing to do with it.

44. For a fuller explanation of the Covenants, see Gordon H. Clark, *The Atonement.* The Trinity Foundation, 1987, 1996.

Wilson writes: "For example [an example of a postulation], God knew and foreordained from before the foundation of the world who the elect would be at the end of the world." Wilson seems to be so taken with the primacy of history that his language suggests that this truth is an assumption, a postulation, we might make, rather than a truth revealed in Scripture. Further, the elect do not emerge at the end of the world-historical process. God knows them from the beginning, because he picked them in eternity, and that number never changes. This is not a postulation that we make; it is a truth revealed in the Bible. God's foreknowledge of elect souls is the *basis* of the Covenant of Grace, not the *result* of the Covenant as it historically unfolds. The Holy Spirit explains that in *Romans* 8:28-30. Wilson writes: "But this foreknowledge [of the elect] is not the covenant itself, but rather God's ultimate knowledge of the outcome of the covenant." Wilson stuffs a straw man into the first part of his sentence so his readers will more readily accept his false conclusion, namely, that foreknowledge is "God's ultimate knowledge of the outcome of the covenant." When God foreknows, he does not look down through the corridors of time to discern what the outcome of the Covenant will be. God's foreknowledge of the elect is God's choosing his people, individual by individual, name by name, by Christ the Mediator, before time and creation begin. The purpose of the Covenant of Grace is the salvation of these people. Creation and redemptive history are the execution of God's eternal plan, whose outcome is absolutely infallible. God does not learn anything by observing outcomes. He knows all history and all outcomes because he planned them, before creation, in divine detail. God implemented his Covenant of Grace to guarantee the salvation of the individuals he chose before the foundation of the world. History, salvation, and the Covenant of Grace are grounded in the decree of God. The theory, the theology, the plan, the doctrine came first, both logically and chronologically. History depends on God's plan; God's plan does not depend on history.

Wilson continues: "But since we know that God has this knowledge [of the elect], we have assumed that this is the 'true' covenant made between God in His secret counsels and the elect, whoever *they* are" (64; the scornful emphasis is Wilson's). There are almost as many falsehoods in this sentence as there are phrases.

Wilson asserts that "we have assumed that this is the 'true' covenant." This is not an assumption, but the teaching of Scripture. In *John* 17 Christ asserts that he has "finished the work" that God the Father had given him to do; that he has "manifested your name to the men whom you have given me out of the world." Christ prays for them; he "does not pray for the world, but for those that you have given me, and none of them is lost." Christ "does not pray for these alone, but also for those who will believe in me through their word" and so on. In this passage Christ tells us plainly that (1) God the Father had given him work to do; (2) that he had in fact accomplished that work; (3) that the Father had picked certain men; (4) that the Father had given these men to Christ; (5) that Christ had infallibly given them the Father's actual words (not analogies of the truth or analogical truths); (6) that the men were saved ("none of them is lost"); and (7) that Christ now requests the promised reward for his completed work. All the characteristics of a covenant of works are present: work assigned; assignment accepted; assignment accomplished; reward expected and given. Christ is the covenant keeper, the only man who has ever kept God's covenant. Christ, acting as the substitute for and representative of his people, has fully met the Father's expectations and fulfilled all righteousness. It is because of Christ's fulfillment of this Covenant of Works that the Covenant of Grace (already quoted above from *Jeremiah* and *Hebrews*) is fulfilled.

Notice that Wilson puts the word "true" in quotation marks. He is not quoting anything; he does this in order to show that he does not believe that the Covenant of Grace (or, for that matter, the Covenant of Works that Christ fulfilled) to be the true covenant. He substitutes a different covenant for both the Covenant of Works and the Covenant of Grace revealed in Scripture.

Notice also that there is no mediator in Wilson's objective covenant. Wilson's objective covenant is made between God and the baptized, not between God the Father and the Lord Jesus Christ, who is the representative of and substitute for the elect. Wilson denigrates the "elect" with his phrase, "whoever *they* are." Wilson contemns the doctrine of individual election taught in Scripture, because he cannot see it. Election is not visible (though its effects may be), and only visible things are "objective" in Wilson's world. That is why he desires to substitute "corporate election" (which is not election to salvation at all) for Biblical election. Being a sensate, earthy man, with his mind set on things below, Wilson demands visibility: "The covenants are historical and visible. Covenants of God have a physical aspect, like an oak tree" (64). But neither the Covenant of Redemption (between the persons of the Trinity), nor the Covenant of Works (between God and the First and Second Adams), nor the Covenant of Grace (between God the Father and Jesus Christ as the representative of the elect) is visible. None of them has a "physical aspect like an oak tree." They are not brown, tall, rough, or twisted. They are not rooted in history, let alone in dirt. When Wilson speaks of his covenant, he is not describing any covenant of Scripture. He is describing his Antichristian medieval religion.

Wilson's counterfeit covenant differs from the Covenant of Grace in many ways:

1. Wilson's covenant has no effective head or mediator, and each sinner is required to fulfil the terms of Wilson's covenant on his own behalf.

2. All who are baptized (or circumcised) are members of Wilson's covenant.

3. Ritual baptism really and spiritually unites all the baptized with Christ in Wilson's covenant.

4. In Wilson's covenant, God makes promises of eternal life and salvation to all who are baptized.

5. If a baptized person to whom God has promised life and salvation does not meet the conditions of the objective covenant, he receives the curses of the objective covenant, and is sent to Hell.

14. The Church Tangible and Intangible

Wilson also attacks the Scriptural and Confessional doctrine of the invisibility of the church. First he trivializes and ridicules the doctrine: "Even in a local assembly there are aspects of the congregation which are invisible as well – emotions, thoughts, and the underside of the pew" (69). We were not aware that pews – let alone their undersides – were "aspects of the congregation." Wilson, in his sensate way, confuses the congregation with furniture. Many other people confuse the local church with a building, or even with organizations that claim to be churches. We realize, of course, that Wilson is attempting to be witty and clever. But his puerile attempt betrays a confusion that lies at the heart of his medieval religion. Furthermore, the underside of pews is not invisible. Wilson seems to be using the word "invisible" in a novel way that would make all sorts of visible things "invisible": the back of your head, New York City, and the far side of the moon, to name only three. In Wilson's world everything visible is also invisible, depending on one's perspective.

Since Wilson thinks that there are "aspects of the congregation" that are invisible, why does he inveigh against the idea of the invisibility of the church? The answer seems to be that the invisible church involves true invisibility: One cannot see the invisible church by changing physical locations, using mirrors, or sending rockets into space.[45] One "sees" this church only by the mind, and Wilson is vehemently opposed to any significant role for the intellect and knowledge in religion. He regards that as "gnosticism." Wilson argues that the Confessional distinction between the visible and invisible church is un-Biblical and that we should think of the church as one (visible) body – Christ's visible body – with members who are faithful to the terms of the covenant and members who are not, but all of whom are genuinely united to Christ by baptism. (In Wilson's ecclesiology, all those in the organized church are in the covenant, and vice versa.) He replaces election and regeneration, which are invisible, with ritual baptism – which is visible; he replaces faith – which is invisible – with works – which are visible; and "final salvation" is granted or withheld, according to one's visible obedience.

Wilson uses this occasion to insinuate that "Hellenism," "which tends to see the ethereal, spiritual realm as the 'real' one" (70) is to blame for much that has gone wrong in theology, including the notion of the invisible church. Now the charge that Greek philosophy unduly influenced Christian theology is not a new one; it has been made for centuries.

45. This reminds one of the story of an early Soviet cosmonaut, who, like Wilson, thought that things invisible were not objective. Upon his return from space he informed the world that he had not seen God out there. To which a Christian replied: If he had opened his space capsule window, he would have.

Eighty years ago J. Gresham Machen wrote a book denying extra-Biblical sources of Paul's theology: *The Origin of Paul's Religion*. The Jehovah's Witnesses tell us, with as much evidence as Wilson cites, that Greek philosophy is the source of the doctrine of the Trinity; and other cultists, including Liberal academics and clerics, have railed against the pagan "Greek mind's" deleterious influence on Christian theology, in opposition to the "Hebrew mind." Wilson is simply echoing these voices.

There was only one significant school of thought in ancient Greece – Plato's, which was soon enough hijacked by the Skeptics – that even comes close to what Wilson mistakenly attributes to "Hellenism" in general. The Epicureans, Democriteans, Aristotelians, Stoics, Sophists, and Greek culture generally were this-worldly. That is why the Olympic Games were a Greek institution (and why the games were revived at the end of the materialist nineteenth century), why Greek statuary largely consists of nudes of buff bodies, and why Greek gods were fraternity boys (and frat boys are Greeks). To say that the Greeks were primarily concerned with the spiritual is to misunderstand intellectual history altogether.

Wilson's comment discloses that he does not understand Christianity either, for it is Christianity, not Hellenism, that "tends to see the eternal, spiritual realm as the 'real' one." Christianity sees the visible world as passing away – as ephemeral. Wilson ignores or perhaps has forgotten the relevant verses, so we will take the time to quote a few here for the benefit of any reader who has been bamboozled by Wilson's (and others') glib perversion of intellectual history and Christian theology:

> Even though our outward man is perishing, yet the inward man is being renewed day by day. For our light affliction, which is but for a moment, is working for us a

> far more exceeding and eternal weight of glory, while we do not look at the things which are seen, but at the things which are not seen. For the things which are seen are temporary, but the things which are not seen are eternal [2 *Corinthians* 4:16-18].

This passage, of course, not only destroys Wilson's perversion of Christianity, it destroys his entire sensate epistemology, which holds that invisible things are not objective. Paul and the Holy Spirit say that visible things are ephemeral, but "the things which are not seen are eternal."

> For if he [our High Priest] were on Earth, he would not be a priest, since there are priests who offer the gifts according to the law; who serve the copy and shadow of the heavenly things, as Moses was divinely instructed when he was about to make the tabernacle... [*Hebrews* 8:4-5].
>
> But Christ came as High Priest of the good things to come, with the greater and more perfect tabernacle not made with hands, that is, not of this creation.... Therefore it was necessary that the copies of the things in the heavens should be purified with these, but the heavenly things themselves with better sacrifices than these. For Christ has not entered the holy places made with hands, which are copies of the true, but into Heaven itself, now to appear in the presence of God for us [*Hebrews* 9:11, 23-24].

The author of *Hebrews,* contradicting Wilson, says that the "true" things are those that are in Heaven, that they are "greater" and "more perfect," and that visible things are "copies" and "shadows" of the "true" things.

> Now faith is the substance of things hoped for, the evidence of things not seen.... By faith we understand

> that the worlds were framed by the Word of God, so that the things which are seen were not made of things which are visible [*Hebrews* 11:1, 3].

Not by sight, but by faith we understand.

How does Wilson apply his earthy, sensate philosophy to the doctrine of the invisible church? He writes: "There is a religious version of this [Hellenism] about, and this is the attitude which sees the 'invisible' Church as the 'true' Church and the 'visible' Church, at best, as only an approximation of the true Church" (70). Wilson does not think the visible church is an approximation of the "true church"; he thinks it is *identical* to the true church. Compare his view to that of J. C. Ryle, who cannot be accused of being a Baptist:

> The church of our text [*Matthew* 16:18] is no material building. It is no temple made with hands, of wood, or brick, or stone, or marble. It is a company of men and women. It is no particular visible church on Earth. It is not the Eastern Church or the Western Church. It is not the Church of England or the Church of Scotland – much less is it the Church of Rome. The church of our text is one that makes far less show in the eyes of man, but is of far more importance in the eyes of God.
>
> The church of our text is made up of all true believers[46] in the Lord Jesus Christ. It comprehends all who have repented of sin, and fled to Christ by faith, and been made new creatures in him. It comprises all God's elect, all who have received God's grace, all who have been washed in Christ's blood, all who have been clothed in Christ's righteousness, all who have been born again and sanctified by Christ's spirit. All such, of every nation, and people, and tongue, compose the church of our text....

46. Notice that the church is composed of believers, not the baptized.

> This is that church to which all visible churches on Earth are servants and handmaidens.... They are the scaffolding, behind which the great building is carried on. They are the husk, under which the living kernel grows. They have their varying degrees of usefulness. The best and worthiest of them is that which trains up most members for Christ's true church.[47]

Or consider Calvin:

> Surely the church of Christ has lived and will live so long as Christ reigns at the right hand of his Father. It is sustained by his hand; defended by his protection; and is kept safe through his power. For he will surely accomplish what he once promised: that he will be present with his own even to the end of the world. Against this church we now have no quarrel. For, of one accord with all believing folk,[48] we worship and adore one God, and Christ the Lord, as he has always been adored by all godly men. But they stray very far from the truth when they do not recognize the church unless they see it with their very eyes,[49] and try to keep it within limits to which it cannot at all be confined.
>
> Our controversy turns on these hinges: First they [the opponents of the Reformers, the Roman Catholics] contend that the form of the church is always apparent and observable. Secondly, they set this form in the see of the Roman Church and its hierarchy. We, on the contrary, affirm that the church can exist without any visible appearance, and that its appearance is not contained within that outward magnificence which they foolishly admire. Rather, it has quite another mark: namely, the pure

47. J. C. Ryle, "The True Church," *The Church Effeminate*, John Robbins, editor. The Trinity Foundation, 2001, 95.

48. Calvin does not say "baptized folk."

49. Calvin is referring to men like Wilson.

> preaching of God's word and the lawful administration of the sacraments. They rage if the church cannot always be pointed to with the finger. But among the Jewish people how often was it so deformed that no semblance of it remained? What form do we think it displayed when Elijah complained that he alone was left? How long after Christ's coming was it hidden without form? How often has it since that time been so oppressed by wars, seditions, and heresies that it did not shine forth at all? If they lived at that time, would they have believed that any church existed? But Elijah heard that there still remained seven thousand men who had not bowed the knee before Ba'al. And we must not doubt that Christ has reigned on Earth ever since he ascended into Heaven. But if believers had then required some visible form, would they not have straightway lost courage?.... Rather, since the Lord alone "knows who are his," let us leave to him the fact that he sometimes removes from men's sight the external signs by which the church is known.[50]

Wilson's view of the church is not, and has never been, the view of Reformed theology.

Wilson writes: "When you have two churches existing at the same time, with the membership lists not identical, this creates a problem." Why is that? Because, Wilson says, "We know there is only one Church." We do? And how do we know that? There are thousands of organized churches in the world, are there not? And are they not as visible and photographable as Wilson could desire? Moreover, the various epistles of the New Testament are addressed to the church at Corinth, to the church at Thessalonica, to the church in Philemon's house, and so on. John writes to the seven churches, plural, which are

50. *Institutes of the Christian Religion,* John T. McNeill, editor. The Westminster Press, 24-26. Quoted in *The Church Effeminate,* 12-13.

in Asia. Moreover these churches are all *visible* churches, just the sort of church that Wilson ought to like. But he ignores all this, contradicts himself, and asserts, after attacking the idea of the invisible church as so much ethereal Greek philosophy, that "there is only one Church."

We hope the reader understands what Wilson is doing. Let us explain. The idea Wilson damns as "Hellenistic" – one invisible church that transcends space and time – he cannot do without. Nominalists[51] such as Wilson must use the "ethereal" concepts they denounce in order to think at all.[52] But though Wilson needs the idea of one church, he cannot admit that it is invisible, for that would destroy his whole cockamamie scheme about the "objectivity of the covenant." He wants – he must – maintain that this one church is visible, and that it is the true church, not an approximation of the true, not a copy or shadow of the true. If his covenant, whose members are all baptized persons, is to be "objective," they must constitute the church. His theory requires him to say that there can be only one church, and that this church is visible. It includes all persons baptized in the name of the Trinity by "an authorized representative of the Christian church."

Wilson's false theology ties him up in contradictions. Earlier he had asserted that there was a problem if there were two churches with differing membership lists. Which one is the real church, he asked? But now, as an alternative to the visible/invisible distinction, he offers us his own two-church theory, the "historical church" and the "eschatological church," whose membership lists differ from each other. If different membership lists created a problem for the invisible/visible

51. See Douglas Wilson, "The Great Logic Fraud," *The Paideia of God*. Canon Press, 1999.

52. See Gordon H. Clark, *Three Types of Religious Philosophy*. The Trinity Foundation, 1973, 1989.

church distinction, they also create a problem for Wilson's historical/eschatological church distinction. Furthermore, Wilson writes, *mirabile dictu*, that "we lose the communion of the saints if we depend on what we can see" (71). But for the previous 70 pages Wilson has been touting visibility as the criterion for objectivity.

Wilson slogs on, apparently oblivious to the mounting contradictions:[53]

> A problem is created when we affirm a belief in two Churches *at the same moment in time*, one visible and the other invisible. Are they the same Church or not? If they are, then why are "membership rosters" different? If they are not, then which is the true church? We know that Christ has only one bride. The natural supposition is that the invisible church, made up of the elect, is the true church. But this leads to a disparagement of the visible church...[74].

Let's apply Wilson's dilemma to the inspired statements in *Hebrews*, that the things on Earth are copies and shadows of things in Heaven. Apparently the writer of *Hebrews*, unlike Wilson, had no problem with saying this. He in fact believed in two tabernacles *at the same moment in time* – just as we believe we have two fathers, one heavenly and one earthly, *at the same moment in time*, and two mothers, one earthly and the New Jerusalem in Heaven.[54] The proper question is not, Which church is real, for both are. The visible church is a real approximation, to use Wilson's own word, of the invisible

53. There is always the possibility that Wilson is not oblivious to the contradictions, but thinks that they are a mark of truth.

54. Incidentally, this disposes of Wilson's asinine analogy and question: "If someone were to tell me that I had a scriptural duty to honor my mother, I should not respond by asking whether he meant my visible mother or my invisible mother.... He simply means my mother..." (72). Furthermore, many people have more than two visible mothers: birth mothers, mothers-in-law, adoptive mothers.

church. Their membership rosters differ because, as both Augustine and Calvin said, there are many wolves within and many sheep without the churches. There are also false brethren, false prophets, and false teachers within the organized churches. There are saved and unsaved (even in churches that do not baptize infants), elect and reprobate in the churches. This means that the visible church – to say nothing of organizations that claim to be churches but are not, such as the enormous Roman and Greek Catholic cults, Liberal Protestant societies, and state bureaucracies such as the Church of England – is indeed inferior to the invisible church, which is unsullied by false professors or false teaching within her pale.

Wilson implies that he does not want to "disparage" the visible church. If we were confident that Wilson is using the phrase "visible church" as the *Westminster Confession* defines it – "all those throughout the world that profess the true religion, together with their children" – we would agree that the visible church is not to be disparaged. But Wilson has another meaning in mind for the phrase "visible church," for he intends to include within that category any organization that claims to be a church and baptizes in the name of the Trinity.

This creates some further difficulty. Wilson writes: "The Church cannot have an earthly head, but only the Lord Jesus Christ as head" (77). Of course, he gives no reason for this statement. One must ask why he uses a distinction – earthly *versus* heavenly – that he has jettisoned. His ecclesiastical categories are "historical" and "eschatological," not earthly and heavenly. And within these new categories, why cannot, why should not, the historical church have an historical head? Wilson has told us many times: Visible good; invisible bad. If so, the visible, historical church ought to have a visible, historical head, and he can be the visible, historical Vicar of Christ, who in the eschaton will turn his visible, historical throne over to Christ himself, when and if Christ becomes visible.[55]

While discussing the head of the church, Wilson declares that removing the language about the pope being Antichrist from the *Westminster Confession* was an "improvement," for it "opens the way for a preterist understanding of prophecy" (77). The *Westminster Confession*, rather than being preterist, was, of course, based on the historical understanding of prophecy developed by the Reformers. Wilson rejects this Reformed view of prophecy and wants to revise the *Confession* to reflect preterism.[56]

Wilson devotes a chapter (9) to the marks of the church, which he puts in Latin ("Notae Ecclesiae"). As Dr. Gordon Clark said, a writer should always remember to use Latin, because it makes one seem so learned. We have tried to do so in this book, imitating Wilson. Wilson opens chapter 9 with a discussion of the "boundaries of the covenant." This is curious for two reasons. First, he has not yet discussed the parties to his covenant, the mediator of his covenant, the content of his covenant, or the maker of his covenant. Apparently he regards the matter of boundaries as more important than those other matters. Second, Wilson identifies, again without argument, the organized churches with his covenant. The boundaries of his covenant are the boundaries of the church, and vice versa. He writes, "If the covenant is not a category invisible to man, then by what marks are we to know it?.... On what scriptural basis do we say that this group is within the covenant, that group outside, and the other group is off sitting in the gray areas?" (79).

55. We must say "if," for preterism is always an option for this medieval religion, and Wilson is sympathetic to this view.

56. See "Antichrist," *The Trinity Review*, October-December 1994; reprinted in *Against the Churches*, John W. Robbins, editor. The Trinity Foundation, 2002, 255-264.

Our first question is: How can there be gray areas in Wilson's objective covenant? The purpose of his insisting that his covenant is visible and objective was to eliminate those fuzzy areas allegedly resulting from the "Greek" notion of an ethereal, invisible church and covenant. Wilson promised us clarity. In Wilson's scheme, individuals and groups were supposed to be clearly (photographably) inside or outside the objective covenant. But now he tells us that gray areas remain. This reminds one of the early boast of the Reconstructionists that they were going to clear up all the confusion about which Mosaic laws still remained in force today by insisting that they all do. They even coined a phrase to express their view: "the abiding validity of the law in exhaustive detail." They said that the distinctions between moral, ceremonial, and judicial laws were illegitimate, for they were all God's law, and God never changes. Then when it finally dawned on some of them what their doctrine implied, they started retreating from their clear but heretical position, and proceeded to tie themselves up in contradictions.[57] Here, with the mention of "gray areas," Wilson withdraws that clarity, that photographability, that he had promised us in his "objective covenant."

As we mentioned earlier, Wilson has difficulty understanding some crucial texts of Scripture. Here his deficiency appears again, for he asserts, based on his misunderstanding of *Galatians* 1, that "Apostles could conceivably fall away and preach a gospel other than the one that Paul preached to the Galatians at the first" (79). Paul's words, which are clearly hypothetical (introduced by an "if" in verses 8 and 9), state or imply no such thing. Apostles, who are divinely appointed

57. See John Robbins, "Theonomic Schizophrenia," *The Trinity Review*, February 1992; reprinted in *Against the Churches: The Trinity Review 1989-1998*, 122-126; and "Will the Real Greg Bahnsen Please Stand Up?" *The Trinity Review*, August 1992; reprinted in *Against the Churches*, 153-157.

teachers, no more than angels from Heaven, could fall away from the Gospel and preach some other message. But Wilson, please keep in mind, has already kicked the doctrine of perseverance into the ether, and it plays no part in his exposition of his objective covenant. Unlike the Apostle Paul, Wilson finds that the doctrine of election and perseverance just gets in the way, rather than explains God's covenant. Furthermore, Wilson misinterprets *Galatians* 1 in order to support the falsehood that the elect can fall away. He seems reluctant to admit that there is a hypothetical warning about anything anywhere in Scripture.[58]

"The Church," Wilson opines, "consists of those who have been called out of darkness and into the light" (83). Is this calling effectual? He says as much: "The Scriptures teach that the gospel creates *life*. And where this life has been created, you have the Church, necessarily connected to her Head. The seed that brings life is the Word.... The seed that brings life is the gospel preached....'being born again, not of corruptible seed, *but of incorruptible, by the Word of God*'" (82). It would follow, then, that the church is all those, and only those, who have been born again. Wilson says as much: "If a man has no faith, then all he has is words, water, and a tiny meal – along with all the curses of the covenant. But if a man sees him [Christ] by faith [!], then when he looks around, he is part of the Church" (83). In this paragraph, Wilson lapses into an almost Christian view of the Gospel and the sacraments – a

58. The phrase "hypothetical warning" is somewhat misleading. The warning in *Galatians* 1 (and other warnings in Scripture) is an actual warning, not hypothetical. Paul uses an impossible event – an angel from Heaven preaching a false gospel – to warn his readers emphatically and dramatically about an actual possibility: that some beings appearing to be and claiming to be angels from Heaven will preach a false gospel. The so-called "hypothetical warnings" in *Hebrews* are similar: The author uses an impossible event – the apostasy of the elect – to give a warning about a real danger – the apostasy of baptized professors and churchgoers, who appear for a while to be genuine Christians, rejecting the truth to perdition.

view that contradicts his dominant view, that ritual baptism, not belief of the Gospel, makes Christians; that words, even if they are true, are dead; and that the sacraments save. Here Wilson seems to say, correctly, that one may be baptized and be lost, and that what makes the difference between salvation and damnation is the Gospel and faith. But perhaps he is using these terms in new ways as well.

Wilson follows this with a chapter on sacerdotalism, saying that "misunderstanding about what actually constitutes sacerdotalism is at the heart of the controversy over the objectivity of the covenant" (85). But Wilson himself doesn't know what the word means, confusing it with sacramentalism. Then, following James Jordan and the Antichristian Peter Leithart,[59] Wilson uses two chapters to slander B. B. Warfield.[60]

Wilson again compares "membership in the Christian faith" with marriage, and, as we pointed out above, this is a recurring analogy throughout the book.

> [T]here is no such thing as a merely nominal Christian any more than we can find a man who is a nominal husband. There are many faithless husbands, but if a man is a husband at all, then he is as much a husband as a faithful one. He is a covenant breaker, but this is not the same as saying that he has no covenant to break. In the same way, there are multitudes of faithless Christians, who do not believe what God said at their baptism [96].

Wilson's analogy is misleading and contradictory. Notice that he frames the analogy by speaking of "membership in the

59. We call Leithart Antichristian because of his recent book, *Against Christianity.*

60. Wilson, in his usual puerile fashion, accuses Warfield of "refried gnosticism" (86). *Gnosticism* is one of Wilson's favorite words, but he doesn't know what it means. That doesn't stop him from accusing anyone who disagrees with his heretical theology of being gnostic.

Christian faith." He does not say membership in the "covenant" or "church," but "membership in the Christian faith." After this flourish, he concludes by speaking of "faithless Christians." So these persons are not "members of the Christian faith" after all? Or are we to understand that "faithless Christians are members of the Christian faith"? Or perhaps Wilson is using "faith" as a synonym for "covenant" or "church"? What makes him think they are equivalent? In *Christian* theology, the word "faith" is not a synonym for either "church" or "covenant." In Wilson's theology it may be. Who knows? Who can know? Wilson uses words to mean whatever he pleases.

The phrase "faithless Christian" is a contradiction in terms, and a "nominal Christian" is a person who acts like, but is not, a Christian – the sort of hypocritical church member James discusses in *James* 2. Similarly, a "nominal husband" (another of Wilson's phrases) is a man who acts like, but is not, a husband – he is a fornicator. He acts in some respects – but not the defining respect – as though he were a husband, but the law does not support his claim and condemns his action. Wilson's denial of the class "nominal husband," implies that all fornicators are husbands, just as his denial of "nominal Christian" implies that all hypocrites are Christians. But the Bible speaks of "false brethren," "false teachers," and "false prophets," all of whom are nominal Christians.

Wilson's rejection of the notion of the church invisible, which he ridicules as the "ethereal church" (21), puts him at odds with the very *Confession* he claims to defend: "The catholic or universal church, which is invisible, consists of the whole number of the elect that have been, are, or shall be gathered into one, under Christ the head thereof; and is the spouse, the body, the fullness of him that fills all in all" (*WCF* 20.5). It is this relationship between the invisible church and individual election that Wilson seeks to sever. He does this by denying the first, the invisible church, and relegating the second, election, to an unknowable realm. The covenant, he asserts, is not with the elect, but with the baptized. Wilson writes: "A true son is brought into the covenant and is nourished there. A false son is brought into the covenant and by his unbelief incurs the chastisements of that covenant. Objectively both the true and false sons are brought into *the same relation*.... Objectively, baptism makes me a member of Christ's body...." (96).[61] Notice that both true and false sons have the "same relation" to Christ.

But the Scriptures and the Westminster Standards disagree:

> Q. 92 What is a sacrament?
> A. A sacrament is an holy ordinance instituted by Christ; wherein, by sensible signs, Christ, and the benefits of the new covenant, are *represented, sealed, and applied to believers.*

Christ and his benefits are represented, sealed, and applied to believers, not to all recipients of a sacrament. Had the Westminster Assembly wished to teach Wilson's objective covenant, they would not have written "believers," but "recipients." This is one of those embarrassing statements in the Standards that Wilson does not discuss. Wilson is correct when he states that nonbelievers add to their own judgment through receiving the sacraments, but it does not follow from this that nonbelievers are members of the Covenant of Grace any more than it follows that a man who engages in sexual intercourse is married to his partner. A fornicator remains a fornicator – he does not become a husband – by participating in some of the activities of a husband. And he faces greater judgment because he does so, precisely because he is *not* married to – *not* in covenant with – his partner.

61. Wilson is quoting Peter Leithart.

Here is another statement from the *Westminster Confession* that Wilson ignores:

> 28.6 The efficacy of baptism is not tied to that moment of time wherein it is administered; yet notwithstanding, by the right use of this ordinance, the grace promised is not only offered, but really exhibited and conferred by the Holy Ghost, *to such (whether of age or infants) as that grace belongs unto, according to the counsel of God's own will, in his appointed time.*

Grace is promised, offered, and conferred only to those "as that grace belongs unto, according to the counsel of God's own will," that is, to his people, his elect. Christian baptism does not offer or confer grace on the reprobate. The Covenant of Grace is with the elect alone. Wilson ignores the statements in the *Larger Catechism* (QQ. 30 and 31) and the Scriptures that support them in his book. Those who are in the Covenant of Grace are those who have been brought into "an estate of salvation." There is and can be no Covenant of Grace with the reprobate. Wilson will look in vain to find such a covenant in the Scriptures or in the Standards which he claims to uphold.

What Wilson seems to be doing, whether he realizes it or not, is working out some implications of John Murray's so-called free offer of the Gospel, which holds that God desires the salvation even of the reprobate.[62] But the *Confession* says that grace is promised only to those to whom it belongs. Those in the covenant are those God delivers from "spiritual thralldom" (*WLC* 101). Reprobates, even baptized ones, are

62. See Garrett Johnson, "The Myth of Common Grace," *The Trinity Review*, March/April 1987; reprinted in *Against the World: The Trinity Review 1978-1988*, 242-249.

not delivered from their spiritual bondage, hence they are not part of the Covenant of Grace.

In Wilson's theology, God delivers from "spiritual thralldom" all those who have been circumcised under the old covenant or baptized by an authorized representative of the Christian church in the name of the Father, the Son and the Holy Ghost with water in the new. However, if there were any doubt about *WLC* 101, the *Westminster Confession* (7:5) states that while the administration of the Covenant of Grace had various forms, through it all God had only one object in mind: "through the operation of the Spirit, to instruct and build up the elect in faith in the promised Messiah, by whom they had full remission of sins, and eternal salvation." Once again, the *Confession* accurately reflects Scripture when it says that the Covenant relationship is with all those who are "elect in faith in the promised Messiah." There is not and never has been a Covenant of Grace with the reprobate. It is appalling that at this late date, some glib writer who claims to be Reformed can assert that the Covenant of Grace is made with elect and reprobate alike – and be widely believed.

Wilson's departure from the Reformed faith at this point leads to his repudiation through redefinition of other articles of the Christian faith. The logical system of doctrine outlined in the *Confession of Faith* does not shake Wilson from his chosen course. After all, thinking in terms of "system" is characteristic of "Enlightenment" and "rationalist" thought, according to Wilson. For Wilson, "systematic interpretations...*must never be allowed to replace* what the Scriptures say" (54). What this means in practical terms is that when our exegesis of Scripture contradicts what Wilson and company claim is the correct interpretation of Scripture, we must embrace the contradiction and not let some "wooden hermeneutic" (that is, logic) get in our way. One might argue that the Neolegalism and proto-Romanism[63] of Wilson and company are the Vantilian love of paradox come home to roost.[64] With systematics safely sidelined and logic rejected as rationalist, Enlightenment thinking, Wilson is free to improvise: "So again, when someone is baptized in the name of the Father, Son and Holy Spirit, they [*sic*] are ushered into an objective, visible, covenant membership. *Regardless of the state of their heart, regardless of any hypocrisy, regardless of whether or not they mean it, such a person is now a visible saint, a Christian*" (194, emphasis added).

Clearly Wilson cannot distinguish a sign of the covenant from the covenant the sign represents. As a consequence, in Wilson's theology everyone from Judas Iscariot to the pope to the Apostle John is a "visible saint, a Christian." But baptism no more makes a person a Christian than dressing an ape makes it a man.

Baptism is always efficacious, Wilson says: "This consecration really happens [in baptism]. God really does it. His people are genuinely set apart; a visible difference is placed between them and the world. By means of baptism, baptism by *water*, grace and salvation is conferred on the elect" (107, emphasis in the original).

Now, this sentence sounds almost Biblical, but we must remember that Wilson has already redefined "elect." Wilson writes that everyone baptized is a "saint," a "Christian," and "elect." It is important to keep in mind that in Wilson's medieval theology, all terms are redefined: The elect are not those whom God has chosen for salvation, and who will be "finally" saved, but those who have been baptized. As John Barach proclaimed at the Auburn Conference in his lecture, "Covenant

63. Under the influence of Shepherd's theology of covenant, election, and justification, several people have joined the Roman Church-State.

64. See Robert Reymond's "Paradox as a Hermeneutical Category" in his *New Systematic Theology of the Christian Religion*, 103-110.

and Election:" "Who are the elect? This is as visible and obvious as your church membership roll...." The elect in this scheme come in two flavors: the "covenantally elect" and the "specially (or decretally) elect." Once again, the Covenant of Grace is emptied of its Biblical meaning by these men who claim to uphold the covenant. In the Moscow theology what makes a person a Christian is not the divine propositions believed, but holy water, which "confers grace and salvation."

This puts Wilson in a uncomfortable position, because at times even he seems to recognize the absurdity of what he is saying: "Of course there are baptized covenant members who are not individually regenerate. They are the ones who reject what God is offering to them in their baptism. They therefore fall away from the *covenant* and not from election...." (104, emphasis in the original). Could the uselessness – the ineffectiveness – of Wilson's covenant be more obvious? If one falls away from Wilson's covenant, one is not falling from grace, but merely from the covenant. Who needs – who wants? – a covenant that is so graceless and consequently so impotent? It is not the "better covenant" described in Scripture.

In Wilson's theology, "becoming a Christian" means being anointed with holy water, not with the Holy Spirit. In the visible, aqueous anointing, God bestows "grace and salvation" even on those who are ultimately lost. Salvation is something that takes place within this "covenant relationship" lived by those "elected" into the covenant via the water of baptism and who persevere until the end, *i.e.*, the "specially elect." Further, since grace is offered and promised to all who are baptized, conversion becomes the "applied grace of their baptism."

What emerges from Wilson's view of the covenant is that what saves a man is a combination of faith and works. This is where Wilson's "eschatological" view of the church comes into play and where the Romish substance of his objective covenant shows through its Reformed veneer. In baptism (in Wilson's covenant), God imposes obligations on the baptized, and how they fulfill those obligations decides their salvation. Wilson repeatedly tells us this relationship is much like an unfaithful husband who, even while mired in infidelity, still has "all the obligations of marriage." The lesson is: In order to be finally saved, sinners must do their part. Salvation is not the result of Christ's work alone outside of them and on their behalf, but something worked in the church "corporately" as church members persevere and live out their lives in covenantal faithfulness. For Wilson, Christians are saved by fulfilling the conditions of the covenant: "In the historic Protestant view, good works are inseparable from biblical salvation. They are not a condiment to flavor a "raw" justification, but rather are definitionally related to justification...like the terms *husband* and *wife*" (173, emphasis in the original).

As we might expect, Wilson quotes no "historic Protestant" who teaches that our "good works are definitionally related to justification." Wilson expects us to accept this proposition because Wilson says so. In Wilson's theology, good works and justification are equals and correlatives, like husband and wife. Justification is not prior to, nor the cause or ground of sanctification and good works, but an equal and corresponding aspect of salvation. But the Holy Spirit speaking in Scripture says otherwise, and repeatedly exhorts believers to lead holy lives. His argument is, You are already Christians; you have already passed from death to everlasting life; you are already saved; therefore, act like Christians. A typical example of such exhortations is "For you were once darkness, but now you are light in the Lord. Walk as children of light.... And have no fellowship with the unfruitful works of darkness, but rather expose them.... See then that you walk circumspectly, not as fools but as wise, redeeming the time, because the days are evil..." (*Ephesians* 5:8, 15-16). There are dozens of such exhortations. But our acting like Christians does not save us, for we are already saved. The indicative – salvation – logically and chronologically precedes the imperative: Behave as the saved people you are. Our good works are not the condition or ground or instrument of our salvation; our salvation is the condition or ground of our obedience. Works and justification are not related as equals, but as effects to cause. Ideas have consequences. Christian ideas have Christian consequences. Those who believe the Gospel, given the opportunity, will produce good works.

In Wilson's theology, the good news of salvation by belief of the Gospel alone is replaced by the unspecified duties of "covenantal faithfulness" in order to keep the grace and salvation conferred by one's baptism. After all, argues Wilson, returning to his addled analogy, "No one assumes that every husband will automatically have a successful marriage. Nor should we assume that every Christian will go to Heaven." In Wilson's theology some Christians will go to Hell.

Wilson's covenant is not only conditional, but sinners must meet the conditions of salvation. He quotes Randy Booth: "This covenantal act of baptism brings the person into a conditional relationship with God. Individual election is unconditional; but individual election is part of the secret decretal will of God, no 'list' of elect individuals having been revealed" (106). Because the list is secret, the fallacious argument goes, the doctrine of individual election is irrelevant to us here on Earth. In Wilson's reworking of the covenant, not only should the church be thought of as "historic and eschatological," but election should be thought of in these terms too, as is evident from Wilson's quote of Joel Garver's "A Brief Catechesis on Covenant and Baptism": "[I]t is precisely in our *'covenantal' election* that *'special' election* is realized and made known. Thus we should not drive a wedge between 'special' and 'covenantal' elections, for special election simply is covenantal election for those, who by God's sovereign electing grace, persevere. For those who fall away, covenantal *election devolves into reprobation*" (139, emphasis added).

Well, yes, to answer our earlier question, the uselessness of Wilson's objective covenant can indeed be made more obvious, and Garver has done so: "Covenantal election devolves into reprobation."

In Wilson's theology, election and reprobation are not eternal decrees of God made before the foundation of the world, they are states which men enter as a result of their actions under the objective covenant – they are covenantal outcomes. They are made elect by baptism, and reprobate by failing to fulfill the (unspecified) conditions of the objective covenant. Wilson's election and reprobation are conditional and revocable. Each is conditioned on one's performance. Garver makes this idea even clearer as he reshapes the Arminian error (espoused by many Halfway Calvinists) of the "well-meant offer" in terms of the covenant:

> [E]lection is only revealed[65] in and through the covenant. The covenant people are the elect people of God in Christ, the Elect One of God. Sadly, many of those who are among the elect people will turn out to be reprobate through apostasy. Nonetheless, God's purposes stand as he gathers his elect people in and through the covenant. Those who persevere in faith have no one to thank but God in his free and sovereign electing love poured out – salvation is by grace alone. Those who apostatize have no one to blame but themselves for having

65. Presumably Garver means "revealed only."

> squandered God's good gifts.... If someone is in Christ by baptism – united to the Head as a member of the Body – then that person is elect. If that person apostatizes and no longer abides in Christ (like the branches in *John* 15), he is no longer elect in Christ, but is reprobate, should he never repent and return. *Whatever time we abide in Christ is a manifestation of God's electing love for us and faithfulness to us.*[66]

Since God's love extends to the reprobate and elect alike, as both are "in Christ" by virtue of being "covenantally elected" at baptism, it follows that it is not God's eternal and immutable love and hatred which determines election and reprobation. It is not on the basis of Christ alone that God loves his own, for we see that both the elect and reprobate are in covenant relationship with Christ, and this is so regardless of the time we abide in Christ. According to Wilson, "both the true and false son are brought into the same relation" to Christ. So what is the determining factor that separates the sheep from the goats? Wilson explains that "faith in the biblical sense is inseparable from faithfulness.... But when we have faith that works its way out in love, which is the only thing that genuine faith can do, *then the condition that God has set for the fulfillment of His promise has been met*" (186-187, emphasis added). The ones who, through their faithfulness, "meet the condition that God has set for the fulfilment of His promise," become sheep. In the objective covenant in which the sinner meets conditions and fulfills his covenantal obligations, thus qualifying himself for the salvation God has promised, Wilson confuses works with sanctification, and both with justification. Wilson's conditional objective covenant is an

66. Garver, http://www.lasalle.edu/~garver/cateches.htm. Emphasis added.

outright denial of the Covenant of Grace and the doctrine of justification by faith alone:

> Those whom God effectually called he also freely justified; *not by infusing righteousness into them*, but by pardoning their sins, and by accounting and accepting their persons as righteous: *not for any thing wrought in them, or done by them*, but for Christ's sake alone: *not by imputing faith itself, the act of believing, or any other evangelical obedience, to them as their righteousness; but by imputing the obedience and satisfaction of Christ unto them*, they *receiving and resting on him and his righteousness by faith*: which faith they have not of themselves; it is the gift of God [*WCF*, 11:1].

Both the sole condition of God's blessing – perfect obedience – and the fulfillment of God's promises have already been met in Christ.

But in Wilson's theology "evangelical obedience" is a condition which must first be met before the promises of the covenant (which both the reprobate and the elect receive in baptism) can be fulfilled. This explains why most of Wilson's chapter on "The Greatness of Justification by Faith" discusses the role of good works in sanctification.

Wilson's conditional objective covenant turns the Biblical and Reformed doctrine of justification on its head: "The end of the tale is eternal life," Wilson writes. But eternal life is not the end result of a life of covenantal faithfulness; it is a gift God gives to believers at the beginning, from the moment of first belief, and based completely on the covenantal faithfulness of their Savior: "There is therefore *now* no condemnation" and "whosoever believes in him shall not perish" but "has *already* passed from death to life." In Christian theology, Jesus Christ is the complete Savior of his people, not merely a good example. Their good works can be done only because they already and irrevocably possess eternal life.[67]

Wilson quotes Booth again: "Only faithful covenant membership (i.e., those full of faith in the Savior), receive the covenant blessings, *including the blessings of imputed righteousness*" (175, emphasis added). That sentence deserves to be read again. The imputation of Christ's righteousness is *the result of being a faithful covenant member*. Wilson immediately adds, "This is fundamental to the central point of this book. Election is one thing and covenant membership is another." For Wilson it is the conditions of salvation that God sets at baptism that become the dividing line between salvation and damnation: "Those who obligate themselves under the terms of the covenant law to live by faith but then defiantly refuse to believe are cut away" (134). In Wilson's scheme, "breaking covenant occurs because of unbelief, lack of faith, and because of lack of good works" (134), and fulfilling the conditions of the covenant occurs by faith and good works. Wilson rejects the historic Reformed and Biblical view of the Covenant of Grace in which Christ is the Mediator of the covenant and the Savior of his people. The imputation of Christ's righteousness is not contingent upon our "faithful covenant membership," but solely upon Christ's obedience to the will of the Father.[68]

67. "Irrevocably" is, of course, redundant, for if someone possesses eternal life, it is by definition irrevocable. But the deliberate confusion of both language and thought in Wilson's book requires the use of such redundancies.

68. Wilson thinks that one must be baptized in order to break the covenant. He writes: "When you baptize an unrepentant pagan, what you actually get is a covenant-breaker. His baptism now obligates him to live a life of repentance, love and trust, which he is refusing to do" (99). This is nonsense. The pagan was obligated to repent and obey before he was baptized. He was already a covenant-breaker. Christian baptism does not make men covenant-breakers; the immediate imputation of Adam's sin does. Imputation seems to play no role in Wilson's theology.

Perhaps a quotation from A. A. Hodge's commentary on chapter 7 of the *Westminster Confession* would help make clear the similarity between Wilson's theology and the heresy of Arminianism:

> The Arminian view [of the covenant] is that Adam, having lost the promise and incurred the penalty of the covenant which demanded perfect obedience, Christ's death having made it consistent with the claims of absolute justice, God for Christ's sake introduces a new covenant, styled the Covenant of Grace, offering to all men individually the eternal life forfeited by Adam on the lowered and graciously possible condition of faith and evangelical obedience. According to this view, the new covenant is just as much a covenant of works as the old one was; the only difference is that the works demanded are far less difficult, and we are graciously aided in our endeavors to accomplish them. According to this view, also, faith and evangelical obedience secure eternal life in the new covenant in the same way that perfect obedience did in the old covenant.
>
> This view is plainly inconsistent with the nature of the Gospel. The method of salvation presented in the Gospel is no compromise of principle, no lowering of terms. Christ fulfills the old legal covenant absolutely....

Along with the rest of the Gospel, Wilson has forgotten Paul's statement in *Romans* 4:4-5: "Now to the one who works, his wage is not reckoned as a favor, but as what is due. But to the one who does not work, but believes in Him who justifies the ungodly, his faith is reckoned as righteousness...." Notice it is not by our faithfulness, our working, that we are reckoned as righteous. God justifies the ungodly, "who does not work." Moreover, *Romans* 10:3-4 says, *apropos* Wilson's theology, "For not knowing about God's righteousness, and seeking to establish their own, they did not subject themselves to the righteousness of God. *For Christ is the end of the law for righteousness to everyone who believes.*"

15. Church Unity

Wilson denounces "our ungodly denominational system" (117). Since he formed his own denomination, the Confederation of Reformed Evangelicals, this sounds slightly hypocritical. He rationalizes his action and tries to dodge the charge of hypocrisy by saying that "every independent congregation is simply a small denomination" (118), so when two congregations form a denomination, there is actually a net loss of one denomination. Equivocation is Wilson's forté. We too can show that dogs have six legs and no ears, if we call ears legs.

Wilson sustains his confusion for more than 200 pages without apparent effort. He writes: "if the Scripture teaches election [he doesn't tell us whether this election is corporate, decretal, individual, covenantal or some other type he has yet to invent], then this is the 'position' of all churches in principle, regardless of what their denominational documents might say about it" (119). One is stunned at such a statement. If Scripture says something, Wilson says, then that is the position "in principle" of all churches, regardless of what the churches themselves say. Why stop at churches? If Scripture says something, that is the position of all the baptized, regardless of what the baptized themselves say. All churches and all the baptized are already united "in principle." True, they might have different structures, organizations, beliefs, practices, and gods, but they are all, in principle, one. Consequently Wilson asserts that baptisms performed by the Church of Christ, the Roman Church-State, and apostate Protestant churches should be recognized as valid baptisms "in order to be nursed back to health" (120-121). Not only does this make a mockery of Christian baptism, it shows that Wilson is ready, willing, and able to sacrifice a Christian ordinance for ecumenical, visible, ecclesiastical unity.

Wilson believes that "liberals, etc., are certainly part of the visible church" (141). Now Liberals are certainly part of organizations that claim to be churches, but they are no part of the "visible church," if by that phrase one means what the Westminster Standards mean. The *Confession* tells us exactly what the Westminster theologians, whom Wilson claims to be defending, meant by the phrase "visible church": "The visible church, which is also catholic or universal under the Gospel (not confined to one nation, as before, under the law), consists of all those throughout the world that profess the true religion, together with their children..." (*WCF* 25.1). Liberals do not profess the true religion, nor do Romanists, nor Orthodoxists, and they are no part of the visible church, as defined by *Westminster.* They may have large organizations they call churches, but since they do not profess the true religion, nor preach the Gospel, nor rightly administer the sacraments, they are not in the visible church. Here is another instance in which Wilson redefines a term, yet he claims to be defending the original meaning of the *Confession* against its modern misinterpreters.

Because he asserts that Liberals are part of the visible church, Wilson scornfully rejects the Biblical command to "come out from among them [Wilson misquotes it as "her"] and be ye separate" as "individualistic" (141). Wilson rejects "separatism." Again, one must ask, why then did Wilson start his own church and his own denomination? More important, why does Wilson still maintain them as separate institutions? His theology of the church demands that he unite with larger bodies, and since he thinks Liberals are Christians, he should be seeking to join the Presbyterian Church in the USA, or the United Methodist Church, or best of all, the Roman Catholic Church-State. By remaining separate from them, Wilson shows himself to be divisive and schismatic, by his own theology. As if this were not embarrassing enough, Wilson again contradicts himself and his vociferous denial that there are any "nominal Christians": "Since they [Liberals] are clearly not Christians, except in name...." Perhaps studying Latin will help Wilson understand that the English word "nominal" is derived from the Latin word for "name."

Wilson even asserts that "false brothers" are "brothers" : "False brothers should be considered both as brothers and as being false" (151). This is idiotic. It is like saying, Counterfeit money should be considered both money and counterfeit. Or, a *faux* pearl is both *faux* and pearl. It is either-or, either genuine or counterfeit. If it is not genuine, it is neither money nor pearl. Wilson, perhaps because he incorrectly thinks all language is metaphorical, does not understand his own metaphors, including the metaphor "false brother." The metaphor literally means: His claim that he is a Christian brother is false. Augustine explained this metaphor 1600 years ago, but Wilson reads moderns. Biblically, false brothers, false teachers, and false prophets are not brothers, but antichrists, wolves, and goats, not sheep. Just because a wolf is in the sheepfold does not make him a sheep, any more than a person being a member of a church makes him a Christian. But in Wilson's theology, anyone in the sheepfold is a Christian, because he has been baptized.

By being baptized, all persons, including false brothers, false teachers, and wolves, are made genuine members of the objective covenant, Wilson says, and they really receive the blessings and benefits of the covenant. "We must receive everyone who is lawfully baptized [by "an authorized representative of the Christian church"] in the name of the Father, Son, and Holy Ghost as a fellow Christian" (142). They are all members of the objective covenant and ingrafted into Christ. Salvation is theirs to lose.

Because he holds this erroneous view, Wilson misunderstands the greetings in the New Testament epistles. He follows Joel Garver, a prolific Internet theologian, and quotes him with approval: "The entire New Testament, and this is especially clear in the epistles, is written to a covenant community composed of both the elect and the non-elect. Nevertheless, the New Testament consistently addresses those who respond to the covenant promises (elect and non-elect alike) as 'brothers,' 'sisters,' 'sons,' 'forgiven,' 'chosen,' 'children of God,' and so on."

Take a moment to digest these propositions. The non-elect, that is the reprobate, can and do "respond to the covenant promises." The reprobate are not dead in sin; they respond to the covenant promises of life and salvation made to them in baptism. According to Wilson, the New Testament calls the reprobate "children of God," "forgiven," and "chosen." So Paul's greeting in *Ephesians* 1, for example, is to be understood as describing all objective covenant members, all church members, believers and unbelievers, elect and reprobate alike:

> Paul, an apostle of Jesus Christ by the will of God, to
> the saints who are in Ephesus, and faithful in Christ Jesus:

There are two words here that need to be singled out for comment: "saints" and "faithful." Paul is clearly writing to the saints, not to all men in Ephesus. Now the question becomes, how does Paul distinguish the saints from other Ephesians? Does he describe them as "baptized in Christ Jesus," or "church members in good standing," or "members of the objective covenant"? No, Paul describes them as *pistos*, believers. The complete Greek phrase is *pistos en Iesou Xristou*: believers in Jesus Christ. Paul distinguishes the saints from other men by their faith, their belief. Most common English translations use the word "faithful" for *pistos*, but that is both misleading and peculiar English. "Believers in Jesus Christ" makes good English and good sense; "faithful in Jesus Christ" sounds peculiar at best. It is the *pistis*, the belief, of the saints, not their obedience, that Paul mentions. Paul is writing to the believers in Ephesus. He is not writing to the baptized, nor to card-signers, nor altar-call responders, nor to those who have retained their salvation by keeping the covenant. Saints, contrary to Wilson, are not the baptized, but the believers. *Pistos* should be translated "believers" in other epistles as well. Paul continues:

> Grace to you and peace from God our Father and the Lord Jesus Christ.

Paul here pronounces a benediction on these believer-saints. He does not pronounce this benediction on everyone, but only on believers. So should all benedictions be pronounced.

> Blessed be the God and Father of our Lord Jesus Christ, who has blessed us with every spiritual blessing in the heavenly places in Christ...

Paul says that God has blessed "us" – Paul puts himself in the same class as those he greets, believers – with every spiritual blessing in Christ. God does not bless unbelievers and the reprobate with every spiritual blessing in Christ, contrary to Garver and Wilson. To maintain that he does is to twist Christian doctrine beyond all recognition. Yet that is what Wilson does with his doctrine of the objective covenant, and his notion that Paul is greeting elect and reprobate alike in his letters.

> ...just as he chose us in him before the foundation of the world...

Of course, only the saints, the believers, are chosen in Christ, not the baptized or the reprobate. Notice the "us," again.

> ...that we should be holy and without blame before him in love...

Only the elect are chosen to be holy and without blame before him. This clause refers to our justification, not our sanctification. It does not say, that we should *become* holy and blameless, but that we should *be* holy and blameless. Christ's perfect righteousness is imputed to all believers, and only to believers, not to all the baptized, nor to all church members, and certainly not to the reprobate.

> ...having predestined us to adoption as sons by Jesus Christ to himself...

The only adopted sons are those who believe, not those who are baptized or church members. *John* 1:12 says, "But as many as received him [not in baptism, but in belief – read on] to them he gave the right to become children of God, to those who believe in his name." The Holy Spirit did not write, "to those who are baptized in his name," nor "to those who eat the bread and drink the wine in his name." The same idea is also found in *Galatians* 3:26: "For you are all sons of God through belief in Christ Jesus."

> ...according to the good pleasure of his will, to the praise of the glory of his grace, by which he made us accepted in the Beloved.

Only the elect, "us," are made accepted in the beloved – only believers are justified.

> In him we have redemption through his blood, the forgiveness of sins, according to the riches of his grace which he made to abound toward us in all wisdom and prudence...

These blessings of Christ are given only to believers, not to all the baptized: redemption, forgiveness of sins, wisdom, and prudence. The "we" and the "us" refer to the same class of people all the way through the greeting. Paul is not writing to reprobates and unbelievers.

> ...having made known to us the mystery of his will, according to his good pleasure which he purposed in himself, that in the dispensation of the fullness of the times he might gather together in one all things in Christ, both which are in Heaven and which are on Earth – in him. In him also we have obtained an inheritance, being predestined according to the purpose of him who works all things according to the counsel of his will, that we who first trusted in Christ should be to the praise of his glory.

Paul here emphasizes predestination and election, and he mentions belief again: "we who first trusted in Christ." Not "we who first were baptized in Christ," but "trusted in Christ" – an invisible, intellectual act, not a visible, ritual act.

> In him you also trusted, after you heard the Word of truth, the Gospel of your salvation; in whom also, having believed...

Paul then emphasizes the point that he is writing to the saints, who are believers in Christ Jesus: "you also [trusted], after you heard the word of truth – which Paul then describes as "the Gospel of your salvation" – and then he mentions belief again. The saints had heard the truth, the Gospel, a message, good news, information, doctrine, theology, and they believed the message they heard. It is belief of the Gospel that distinguishes the saints in Ephesus from other Ephesians. Paul is not writing to unbelievers or the reprobate in Ephesus. Anyone who says he is hasn't a clue as to what the New Testament is about.

> ...you were sealed with the Holy Spirit of promise, who is the guarantee of our inheritance until the redemption of the purchased possession, to the praise of his glory.

These believers in Christ Jesus to whom Paul is writing are sealed with the Holy Spirit. He, not our faithful obedience, guarantees our inheritance. To argue, as Wilson and his accomplices do, that the greetings of the epistles address a promiscuous group of believers and unbelievers, elect and reprobate, is simply false. It finds no support in the text.

16. Conclusion

On every topic he discusses, Wilson's theology is different from and opposed to the Christian faith. Even when Wilson seems to say something Biblical and true, he contradicts it at another point, and the whole infrastructure of his thought, in which basic Christian terms are redefined, makes his assertions false. His theology is opposed to the system of doctrine taught in Scripture and outlined in the *Westminster Confession of Faith*. He agrees with the prelates at the Council of Trent (who according to his theology are his Christian brothers) who thought propositions without works are dead, who denied that sinners are justified by belief alone, and who affirmed that final salvation is conditioned on the obedience of Christians after their baptism.

Wilson and his friends have rejected all calls for repentance, and they have hardened their hearts and position, which is not Reformed at all. He and his friends should fear the coming judgment of God.

Scripture Index

Index

The Crisis of Our Time

HISTORIANS have christened the thirteenth century the Age of Faith and termed the eighteenth century the Age of Reason. The present age has been called many things: the Atomic Age, the Age of Inflation, the Age of the Tyrant, the Age of Aquarius; but it deserves one name more than the others: the Age of Irrationalism. Contemporary secular intellectuals are anti-intellectual. Contemporary philosophers are anti-philosophy. Contemporary theologians are anti-theology.

In past centuries, secular philosophers have generally believed that knowledge is possible to man. Consequently they expended a great deal of thought and effort trying to justify knowledge. In the twentieth century, however, the optimism of the secular philosophers all but disappeared. They despaired of knowledge.

Like their secular counterparts, the great theologians and doctors of the church taught that knowledge is possible to man. Yet the theologians of the present age also repudiated that belief. They too despaired of knowledge. This radical skepticism has penetrated our entire culture, from television to music to literature. *The Christian at the beginning of the twenty-first century is confronted with an overwhelming cultural consensus – sometimes stated explicitly but most often implicitly: Man does not and cannot know anything truly.*

What does this have to do with Christianity? Simply this: If man can know nothing truly, man can truly know nothing. We cannot know that the Bible is the Word of God, that Christ died for his people, or that Christ is alive today at the right hand of the Father. Unless knowledge is possible, Christianity is nonsensical, for it claims to be knowledge. What is at stake at the beginning of the twenty-first century is not simply a single doctrine, such as the virgin birth, or the existence of Hell, as important as those doctrines may be, but the whole of Christianity itself. If knowledge is not possible to man, it is worse than silly to argue points of doctrine – it is insane.

The irrationalism of the present age is so thoroughgoing and pervasive that even the Remnant – the segment of the professing church that remains faithful – has accepted much of it, frequently without even being aware of what it is accepting. In some religious circles this irrationalism has become synonymous with piety and humility, and those who oppose it are denounced as rationalists, as though to be logical were a sin. Our contemporary anti-theologians make a contradiction and call it a Mystery. The faithful ask for truth and are given Paradox and Antinomy. If any balk at swallowing the absurdities of the anti-theologians who teach in the seminaries or have graduated from the seminaries, they are frequently marked as heretics or schismatics who seek to act independently of God.

There is no greater threat facing the church of Christ at this moment than the irrationalism that now controls our entire culture. Totalitarianism, guilty of tens of millions of murders – including those of millions of Christians – is to be feared, but not nearly so much as the idea that we do not and cannot know the literal truth. Hedonism, the popular philosophy of America, is not to be feared so much as the belief that logic – that "mere human logic," to use the religious irrationalists' own phrase – is futile. The attacks on truth, on knowledge, on propositional revelation, on the intellect, on words, and on logic are renewed daily. But note well: The misologists – the haters of logic – use logic to demonstrate the futility of using logic. The anti-intellectuals construct intricate intellectual arguments to prove the insufficiency of the intellect. Those who deny the competence of words to express thought use words to express their thoughts. The proponents of poetry, myth, metaphor, and analogy argue for their theories by using literal prose, whose competence – even whose possibility – they deny. The anti-theologians use the revealed Word of God to show that there can be no revealed Word of God – or that if there could, it would remain impenetrable darkness and Mystery to our finite minds.

Nonsense Has Come

Is it any wonder that the world is grasping at straws – the straws of experientialism, mysticism, and drugs? After all, if people are told that the Bible contains insoluble mysteries, then is not a flight into mysticism to be expected? On what grounds can it be condemned? Certainly not on logical grounds or Biblical grounds, if logic is futile and the Bible unknowable. Moreover, if it cannot be condemned on logical or Biblical grounds, it cannot be condemned at all. If people are going to have a religion of the mysterious, they will not adopt Christianity: They will have a genuine mystery religion. The popularity of mysticism, drugs, and religious experience is the logical consequence of the irrationalism of the present age. There can and will be no Christian reformation – and no restoration of a free society – unless and until the irrationalism of the age is totally repudiated by Christians.

The Church Defenseless

Yet how shall they do it? The official spokesmen for Christianity have been fatally infected with irrationalism. The seminaries, which annually train thousands of men to teach millions of Christians, are the finishing schools of irrationalism, completing the job begun by the government schools and colleges. Most of the pulpits of the conservative churches (we are not speaking of the obviously apostate churches) are occupied by graduates of the anti-theological schools. These products of modern anti-theological education, when asked to give a reason for the hope that is in them, can generally respond with only the intellectual analogue of a shrug – a mumble about Mystery. They have not grasped – and therefore cannot teach those for whom they are responsible – the first truth: "And you shall know the truth." Many, in fact, explicitly contradict Christ, saying that, at best, we possess only "pointers" to the truth, or something "similar" to the truth, a mere analogy. Is the impotence of the Christian church a puzzle? Is the fascination with Pentecostalism, faith healing, Eastern Orthodoxy, and Roman Catholicism – all sensate and anti-intellectual religions – among members of Christian churches an enigma? Not when one understands the pious nonsense that is purveyed in the name of God in the religious colleges and seminaries.

The Trinity Foundation

The creators of The Trinity Foundation firmly believe that theology is too important to be left to the licensed theologians – the graduates of the schools of theology. They have created The Trinity Foundation for the express purpose of teaching believers all that the Scriptures contain – not warmed over, baptized, Antichristian philosophies. Each member of the board of directors of The Trinity Foundation has signed this oath: "I believe that the Bible alone and the Bible in its entirety is the Word of God and, therefore, inerrant in the autographs. I believe that the system of truth presented in the Bible is best summarized in the *Westminster Confession of Faith.* So help me God."

The ministry of The Trinity Foundation is the presentation of the system of truth taught in Scripture as clearly and as completely as possible. We do not regard obscurity as a virtue, nor confusion as a sign of spirituality. Confusion, like all error, is sin, and teaching that confusion is all that Christians can hope for is doubly sin.

The presentation of the truth of Scripture necessarily involves the rejection of error. The Foundation has exposed and will continue to expose the irrationalism of the present age, whether its current spokesman be an existentialist philosopher or a professed Reformed theologian. We oppose anti-intellectualism, whether it be espoused by a Neo-orthodox theologian or a fundamentalist evangelist. We reject misology, whether it be on the lips of a Neo-evangelical or those of a Roman Catholic Charismatic. We repudiate agnosticism, whether it be secular or religious. To each error we bring the brilliant light of Scripture, proving all things, and holding fast to that which is true.

The Primacy of Theory

The ministry of The Trinity Foundation is not a "practical" ministry. If you are a pastor, we will not enlighten you on how to organize an ecumenical prayer meeting in your community or how to double church attendance in a year. If you are a homemaker, you will have to read elsewhere to find out how to become a total woman. If you are a businessman, we will not tell you how to develop a social conscience. The professing church is drowning in such "practical" advice.

The Trinity Foundation is unapologetically theoretical in its outlook, believing that theory without practice is dead, and that practice without theory is blind. The trouble with the professing church is not primarily in its practice, but in its theory. Churchgoers and teachers do not know, and many do not even care to know, the doctrines of Scripture. Doctrine is intellectual, and churchgoers and teachers are generally anti-intellectual. Doctrine is ivory tower philosophy, and they scorn ivory towers. The ivory tower, however, is the control tower of a civilization. It is a fundamental, theoretical mistake of the "practical" men to think that they can be merely practical, for practice is always the practice of some theory. The relationship between theory and practice is the relationship between cause and effect. If a person believes correct theory, his practice will tend to be correct. The practice of contemporary Christians is immoral because it is the practice of false theories. It is a major theoretical mistake of the "practical" men to think that they can ignore the ivory towers of the philosophers and theologians as irrelevant to their lives. Every action that "practical" men take is governed by the thinking that has occurred in some ivory tower – whether that tower be the British Museum; the Academy; a home in Basel, Switzerland; or a tent in Israel.

In Understanding Be Men

It is the first duty of the Christian to understand correct theory – correct doctrine – and thereby implement correct practice. This order – first theory, then practice – is both logical and Biblical. It is, for example, exhibited in Paul's *Epistle to the Romans,* in which he spends the first eleven chapters expounding theory and the last five discussing practice. The contemporary teachers of Christians have not only reversed the Biblical order, they have inverted the Pauline emphasis on theory and practice. The virtually complete failure of the teachers of the professing church to instruct believers in correct doctrine is the cause of the misconduct and spiritual and cultural impotence of Christians. The church's lack of power is the result of its lack of truth. The *Gospel* is the power of God, not religious experiences or personal relationships. The church has no power because it has abandoned the Gospel, the good news, for a religion of experientialism. Twentieth-first-century American churchgoers are children carried about by every wind of doctrine, not knowing what they believe, or even if they believe anything for certain.

The chief purpose of The Trinity Foundation is to counteract the irrationalism of the age and to expose the errors of the teachers of the church. Our emphasis – on the Bible as the sole source of knowledge, on the primacy of truth, on the supreme importance of correct doctrine, and on the necessity for systematic and logical thinking – is almost unique in Christendom. To the extent that the church survives – and she will survive and flourish – it will be because of her increasing acceptance of these basic ideas and their logical implications.

We believe that The Trinity Foundation is filling a vacuum in Christendom. We are saying that Christianity is intellectually defensible – that, in fact, it is the only intellectually defensible system of thought. We are saying that God has made the wisdom of this world – whether that wisdom be called science, religion, philosophy, or common sense – foolishness. We are appealing to all Christians who have not conceded defeat in the intellectual battle with the world to join us in our efforts to raise a standard to which all men of sound mind can repair.

The love of truth, of God's Word, has all but disappeared in our time. We are committed to and pray for a great instauration. But though we may not see this reformation in our lifetimes, we believe it is our duty to present the whole counsel of God, because Christ has commanded it. The results of our teaching are in God's hands, not ours. Whatever those results, his Word is never taught in vain, but always accomplishes the result that he intended it to accomplish. Professor Gordon H. Clark has stated our view well:

> There have been times in the history of God's people, for example, in the days of Jeremiah, when refreshing grace and widespread revival were not to be expected: The time was one of chastisement. If this twentieth century is of a similar nature, individual Christians here and there can find comfort and strength in a study of God's Word. But if God has decreed happier days for us, and if we may expect a world-shaking and genuine spiritual awakening, then it is the author's belief that a zeal for souls, however necessary, is not the sufficient condition. Have there not been devout saints in every age, numerous enough to carry on a revival? Twelve such persons are plenty. What distinguishes the arid ages from the period of the Reformation, when nations were moved as they had not been since Paul preached in Ephesus, Corinth, and Rome, is the latter's fullness of knowledge of God's Word. To echo an early Reformation thought, when the ploughman and the garage attendant know the Bible as well as the theologian does, and know it better than some contemporary theologians, then the desired awakening shall have already occurred.

In addition to publishing books, the Foundation publishes a monthly newsletter, *The Trinity Review*. Subscriptions to *The Review* are free to U.S. addresses; please write to the address on the order form to become a subscriber. If you would like further information or would like to join us in our work, please let us know.

The Trinity Foundation is a non-profit foundation, tax exempt under section 501 (c)(3) of the Internal Revenue Code of 1954. You can help us disseminate the Word of God through your tax-deductible contributions to the Foundation.

John W. Robbins

Intellectual Ammunition

THE Trinity Foundation is committed to bringing every philosophical and theological thought captive to Christ. The books listed below are designed to accomplish that goal. They are written with two subordinate purposes: (1) to demolish all non-Christian claims to knowledge; and (2) to build a system of truth based upon the Bible alone.

Philosophy

Ancient Philosophy
Gordon H. Clark — Trade paperback $24.95

This book covers the thousand years from the Pre-Socratics to Plotinus. It represents some of the early work of Dr. Clark – the work that made his academic reputation. It is an excellent college text.

Behaviorism and Christianity
Gordon H. Clark — Trade paperback $5.95

Behaviorism is a critique of both secular and religious behaviorists. It includes chapters on John Watson, Edgar S. Singer, Jr., Gilbert Ryle, B. F. Skinner, and Donald MacKay. Clark's refutation of behaviorism and his argument for a Christian doctrine of man are unanswerable.

Christ and Civilization
John W. Robbins — Trade paperback $3.95

Civilization as we know it is a result of the widespread proclamation and belief of the Gospel of justification by faith alone in the sixteenth century. Christ foretold this result in the Sermon on the Mount: "Seek first the Kingdom of God and his righteousness, and all these things will be added to you."

This brief overview of the history of western civilization makes it clear that our cultural debt is to the Gospel, not to Greece and Rome.

A Christian Philosophy of Education Hardback $18.95
Gordon H. Clark Trade paperback $12.95

The first edition of this book was published in 1946. It sparked the contemporary interest in Christian schools. In the 1970s, Dr. Clark thoroughly revised and updated it, and it is needed now more than ever. Its chapters include: The Need for a World-View; The Christian World-View; The Alternative to Christian Theism; Neutrality; Ethics; The Christian Philosophy of Education; Academic Matters; and Kindergarten to University. Three appendices are included: The Relationship of Public Education to Christianity; A Protestant World-View; and Art and the Gospel.

A Christian View of Men and Things Hardback $29.95
Gordon H. Clark Trade paperback $14.95

No other book achieves what *A Christian View* does: the presentation of Christianity as it applies to history, politics, ethics, science, religion, and epistemology. Dr. Clark's command of both worldly philosophy and Scripture is evident on every page, and the result is a breathtaking and invigorating challenge to the wisdom of this world.

Clark Speaks from the Grave
Gordon H. Clark — Trade paperback $3.95

Dr. Clark chides some of his critics for their failure to defend Christianity competently. *Clark Speaks* is a stimulating and illuminating discussion of the errors of contemporary apologists.

Ecclesiastical Megalomania: The Economic and Political Thought of the Roman Catholic Church
John W. Robbins — Hardback $21.95

This detailed and thorough analysis and critique of the social teaching of the Roman Church-State is the only such book available by a Christian economist and political philosopher. The book's conclusions reveal the Roman Church-State to be an advocate of its own brand of faith-based fascism. *Ecclesiastical Megalomania* includes the complete text of the *Donation of Constantine* and Lorenzo Valla's exposé of the hoax.

Education, Christianity, and the State
J. Gresham Machen — Trade paperback $10.95

Machen was one of the foremost educators, theologians, and defenders of Christianity in the twentieth century. The author of several scholarly books, Machen saw clearly that if Christianity is to survive and flourish, a system of Christian schools must be established. This collection of essays and speeches captures his thoughts on education over nearly three decades.

Essays on Ethics and Politics
Gordon H. Clark — Trade paperback $10.95

Dr. Clark's essays, written over the course of five decades, are a major statement of Christian ethics.

Gordon H. Clark: Personal Recollections
John W. Robbins, editor Trade paperback $6.95

Friends of Dr. Clark have written their recollections of the man. Contributors include family members, colleagues, students, and friends such as Harold Lindsell, Carl Henry, Ronald Nash, and Anna Marie Hager.

Historiography: Secular and Religious
Gordon H. Clark Trade paperback $13.95

In this masterful work, Dr. Clark applies his philosophy to the writing of history, examining all the major schools of historiography.

An Introduction to Christian Philosophy
Gordon H. Clark Trade paperback $8.95

In 1966 Dr. Clark delivered three lectures on philosophy at Wheaton College. In these lectures he criticizes secular philosophy and launches a philosophical revolution in the name of Christ.

Language and Theology
Gordon H. Clark Trade paperback $9.95

There were two main currents in twentieth-century philosophy – language philosophy and existentialism. Both were hostile to Christianity. Dr. Clark disposes of language philosophy in this brilliant critique of Bertrand Russell, Ludwig Wittgenstein, Rudolf Carnap, A. J. Ayer, Langdon Gilkey, and many others.

Logic Hardback $16.95
Gordon H. Clark Trade paperback $10.95

Written as a textbook for Christian schools, *Logic* is another unique book from Dr. Clark's pen. His presentation of the laws of thought, which must be followed if Scripture is to be understood correctly, and which are found in Scripture itself, is both clear and thorough. *Logic* is an indispensable book for the thinking Christian.

Lord God of Truth, Concerning the Teacher
Gordon H. Clark and
Aurelius Augustine — Trade paperback $7.95

This essay by Dr. Clark summarizes many of the most telling arguments against empiricism and defends the Biblical teaching that we know God and truth immediately. The dialogue by Augustine is a refutation of empirical language philosophy.

The Philosophy of Science and Belief in God
Gordon H. Clark — Trade paperback $8.95

In opposing the contemporary idolatry of science, Dr. Clark analyzes three major aspects of science: the problem of motion, Newtonian science, and modern theories of physics. His conclusion is that science, while it may be useful, is always false; and he demonstrates its falsity in numerous ways. Since science is always false, it can offer no alternative to the Bible and Christianity.

Religion, Reason and Revelation
Gordon H. Clark — Trade paperback $10.95

One of Dr. Clark's apologetical masterpieces, *Religion, Reason and Revelation* has been praised for the clarity of its thought and language. It includes these chapters: Is Christianity a Religion? Faith and Reason; Inspiration and Language; Revelation and Morality; and God and Evil. It is must reading for all serious Christians.

The Scripturalism of Gordon H. Clark
W. Gary Crampton Trade paperback $9.95

Dr. Crampton has written an introduction to the philosophy of Gordon H. Clark that is helpful to both beginners and advanced students of theology. This book includes a bibliography of Dr. Clark's works.

Thales to Dewey:
A History of Philosophy Hardback $29.95
Gordon H. Clark Trade paperback $21.95

This is the best one-volume history of philosophy in print.

Three Types of Religious Philosophy
Gordon H. Clark Trade paperback $6.95

In this book on apologetics, Dr. Clark examines empiricism, rationalism, dogmatism, and contemporary irrationalism, which does not rise to the level of philosophy. He offers an answer to the question, "How can Christianity be defended before the world?"

William James and John Dewey
Gordon H. Clark Trade paperback $8.95

William James and John Dewey are two of the most influential philosophers America has produced. Their philosophies of instrumentalism and pragmatism are hostile to Christianity, and Dr. Clark demolishes their arguments.

Without A Prayer: Ayn Rand and the Close of Her System
John W. Robbins Hardback $27.95

Ayn Rand has been a best-selling author since 1957. *Without A Prayer* discusses Objectivism's epistemology, theology, ethics, and politics in detail. Appendices include analyses of books by Leonard Peikoff and David Kelley, as well as several essays on Christianity and philosophy.

Theology

Against the Churches: The Trinity Review 1989-1998
John W. Robbins, editor Oversize hardback $39.95

This is the second volume of essays from *The Trinity Review*, covering its second ten years, 1989-1998. This volume, like the first, is fully indexed and is very useful in research and in the classroom. Authors include: Gordon Clark, John Robbins, Charles Hodge, J. C. Ryle, Horatius Bonar, and Robert L. Dabney.

Against the World: The Trinity Review 1978-1988
John W. Robbins, editor Oversize hardback $34.95

This is a clothbound collection of the essays published in *The Trinity Review* from 1978 to 1988, 70 in all. It is a valuable source of information and arguments explaining and defending Christianity.

The Atonement
Gordon H. Clark Trade paperback $8.95

In *The Atonement*, Dr. Clark discusses the covenants, the virgin birth and incarnation, federal headship and representation, the relationship between God's sovereignty and justice, and much more. He analyzes traditional views of the atonement and criticizes them in the light of Scripture alone.

The Biblical Doctrine of Man
Gordon H. Clark Trade paperback $6.95

Is man soul and body or soul, spirit, and body? What is the image of God? Is Adam's sin imputed to his children? Is evolution true? Are men totally depraved? What is the heart? These are some of the questions discussed and answered from Scripture in this book.

By Scripture Alone
W. Gary Crampton Trade paperback $12.95

This is a clear and thorough explanation of the Scriptural doctrine of Scripture and a refutation of the recent Romanist attack on Scripture as the Word of God.

The Changing of the Guard
Mark W. Karlberg Trade paperback $3.95

This essay is a critical discussion of Westminster Seminary's anti-Reformational and un-Biblical teaching on the doctrine of justification. Dr. Karlberg exposes the doctrine of justification by faith and works – not *sola fide* – taught at Westminster Seminary for the past 25 years, by Professors Norman Shepherd, Richard Gaffin, John Frame, and others.

The Church Effeminate
John W. Robbins, editor Hardback $29.95

This is a collection of 39 essays by the best theologians of the church on the doctrine of the church: Martin Luther, John Calvin, Benjamin Warfield, Gordon Clark, J.C. Ryle, and many more. The essays cover the structure, function, and purpose of the church.

The Clark-Van Til Controversy
Herman Hoeksema Trade paperback $7.95

This collection of essays by the founder of the Protestant Reformed Churches – essays written at the time of the Clark-Van Til controversy in the 1940s – is one of the best commentaries on those events in print.

A Companion to The Current Justification Controversy
John W. Robbins Trade paperback $9.95

This book includes documentary source material not available in *The Current Justification Controversy*, an essay tracing the origins and continuation of this controversy throughout American Presbyterian churches, and an essay on the New Perspective on Paul by Robert L. Reymond.

Cornelius Van Til: The Man and The Myth
John W. Robbins Trade paperback $2.45

The actual teachings of this eminent Philadelphia theologian have been obscured by the myths that surround him. This book penetrates those myths and criticizes Van Til's surprisingly unorthodox views of God and the Bible.

The Current Justification Controversy
O. Palmer Robertson Trade paperback $9.95

From 1975 to 1982 a controversy over justification raged within Westminster Theological Seminary and the Philadelphia Presbytery of the Orthodox Presbyterian Church. As a member of the faculties of both Westminster and Covenant Seminaries during this period, O. Palmer Robertson was an important participant in this controversy. This is his account of the controversy, vital background for understanding the defection from the Gospel that is now widespread in Presbyterian churches.

The Everlasting Righteousness
Horatius Bonar Trade paperback $8.95

Originally published in 1874, the language of Bonar's masterpiece on justification by faith alone has been updated and Americanized for easy reading and clear understanding. This is one of the best books ever written on justification.

God and Evil: The Problem Solved
Gordon H. Clark Trade paperback $5.95

This volume is Chapter 5 of *Religion, Reason and Revelation,* in which Dr. Clark presents his solution to the problem of evil.

God-Breathed: The Divine Inspiration of the Bible
Louis Gaussen Trade paperback $16.95

Gaussen, a nineteenth-century Swiss Reformed pastor, comments on hundreds of passages in which the Bible claims to be the Word of God. This is a massive defense of the doctrine of the plenary and verbal inspiration of Scripture.

God's Hammer: The Bible and Its Critics
Gordon H. Clark Trade paperback $10.95

The starting point of Christianity, the doctrine on which all other doctrines depend, is "The Bible alone, and the Bible in its entirety, is the Word of God written, and, therefore, inerrant in the autographs." Over the centuries the opponents of Christianity, with Satanic shrewdness, have concentrated their attacks on the truthfulness and completeness of the Bible. In the twentieth century the attack was not so much in the fields of history and archaeology as in philosophy. Dr. Clark's brilliant defense of the complete truthfulness of the Bible is captured in this collection of eleven major essays.

The Holy Spirit
Gordon H. Clark Trade paperback $8.95

This discussion of the third person of the Trinity is both concise and exact. Dr. Clark includes chapters on the work of the Spirit, sanctification, and Pentecostalism. This book is part of his multi-volume systematic theology that began appearing in print in 1985.

The Incarnation
Gordon H. Clark Trade paperback $8.95

Who is Christ? The attack on the doctrine of the Incarnation in the nineteenth and twentieth centuries was vigorous, but the orthodox response was lame. Dr. Clark reconstructs the doctrine of the Incarnation, building and improving upon the Chalcedonian definition.

The Johannine Logos
Gordon H. Clark Trade paperback $5.95

Dr. Clark analyzes the relationship between Christ, who is the truth, and the Bible. He explains why John used the same word to refer to both Christ and his teaching. Chapters deal with the Prologue to John's Gospel; *Logos* and *Rheemata*; Truth; and Saving Faith.

Justification by Faith Alone
Charles Hodge Trade paperback $10.95

Charles Hodge of Princeton Seminary was the best American theologian of the nineteenth century. Here, for the first time, are his two major essays on justification in one volume. This book is essential in defending the faith.

Karl Barth's Theological Method
Gordon H. Clark Trade paperback $18.95

Karl Barth's Theological Method is perhaps the best critique of the Neo-orthodox theologian Karl Barth ever written. Dr. Clark discusses Barth's view of revelation, language, and Scripture, focusing on his method of writing theology, rather than presenting a comprehensive analysis of the details of Barth's theology.

Logical Criticisms of Textual Criticism
Gordon H. Clark Trade paperback $3.25

Dr. Clark's acute mind enables him to demonstrate the inconsistencies, assumptions, and flights of fancy that characterize the science of New Testament criticism.

Not Reformed at All: Medievalsim in "Reformed" Churches
John Robbins and Sean Gerety Trade paperback $9.95

This book is a response to and refutation of Douglas Wilson's book *"Reformed" is Not Enough: Recovering the Objectivity of the Covenant.*

Wilson, one of the leading figures in the Neolegalist movement in Reformed and Presbyterian circles, attacked covenant theology and proposed a "visible, photographable" covenant which one enters by ritual baptism, making one a Christian. That salvation can be lost by one's own lack of performance or by action of authorized representatives of the church. This refutation of Wilson is a defense of the Covenant of Grace.

Predestination
Gordon H. Clark — Trade paperback $10.95

Dr. Clark thoroughly discusses one of the most controversial and pervasive doctrines of the Bible: that God is, quite literally, Almighty. Free will, the origin of evil, God's omniscience, creation, and the new birth are all presented within a Scriptural framework. The objections of those who do not believe in Almighty God are considered and refuted. This edition also contains the text of the booklet, *Predestination in the Old Testament.*

Sanctification
Gordon H. Clark — Trade paperback $8.95

In this book, which is part of Dr. Clark's multi-volume systematic theology, he discusses historical theories of sanctification, the sacraments, and the Biblical doctrine of sanctification.

Study Guide to the Westminster Confession
W. Gary Crampton — Oversize paperback $10.95

This *Study Guide* can be used by individuals or classes. It contains a paragraph-by-paragraph summary of the *Westminster Confession,* and questions for the student to answer. Space for answers is provided. The *Guide* will be most beneficial when used in conjunction with Dr. Clark's *What Do Presbyterians Believe?*

A Theology of the Holy Spirit
Frederick Dale Bruner — Trade paperback $16.95

First published in 1970, this book has been hailed by reviewers as "thorough," "fair," "comprehensive," "devastating," "the most significant book on the Holy Spirit," and "scholarly." Gordon Clark described this book in his own book *The Holy Spirit* as "a masterly and exceedingly well researched exposition of Pentecostalism. The documentation is superb, as is also his penetrating analysis of their non-scriptural and sometimes contradictory conclusions." Unfortunately, the book is marred by the author's sacramentarianism.

The Trinity
Gordon H. Clark — Trade paperback $8.95

Apart from the doctrine of Scripture, no teaching of the Bible is more fundamental than the doctrine of God. Dr. Clark's defense of the orthodox doctrine of the Trinity is a principal portion of his systematic theology. There are chapters on the Deity of Christ; Augustine; the Incomprehensibility of God; Bavinck and Van Til; and the Holy Spirit; among others.

What Calvin Says
W. Gary Crampton — Trade paperback $10.95

This is a clear, readable, and thorough introduction to the theology of John Calvin.

What Do Presbyterians Believe?
Gordon H. Clark — Trade paperback $10.95

This classic is the best commentary on the *Westminster Confession of Faith* ever written.

What Is Saving Faith?
Gordon H. Clark | Trade paperback $12.95

This is the combined edition of *Faith and Saving Faith* and *The Johannine Logos.* The views of the Roman Catholic Church, John Calvin, Thomas Manton, John Owen, Charles Hodge, and B. B. Warfield are discussed in this book. Is the object of faith a person or a proposition? Is faith more than belief? Is belief thinking with assent, as Augustine said? In a world chaotic with differing views of faith, Dr. Clark clearly explains the Biblical view of faith and saving faith.

In *The Johannine Logos*, Dr. Clark analyzes the relationship between Christ, who is the truth, and the Bible. He explains why John used the same word to refer to both Christ and his teaching. Chapters deal with the Prologue to John's Gospel; *Logos* and *Rheemata;* Truth; and Saving Faith.

Clark's Commentaries on the New Testament

Colossians	Trade paperback	$6.95
Ephesians	Trade paperback	$8.95
First Corinthians	Trade paperback	$10.95
First John	Trade paperback	$10.95
First and Second Thessalonians	Trade paperback	$5.95
New Heavens, New Earth (*First* and *Second Peter*)	Trade paperback	$10.95
The Pastoral Epistles	Hardback	$29.95
(*1* and *2 Timothy* and *Titus*)	Trade paperback	$14.95
Philippians	Trade paperback	$9.95

All of Clark's commentaries are expository, not technical, and are written for the Christian layman. His purpose is to explain the text clearly and accurately so that the Word of God will be thoroughly known by every Christian.

The Trinity Library

We will send you one copy of each of the 60 books listed above for $500 (retail value $800), postpaid to any address in the U.S. You may also order the books you want individually on the order form on the next page. Because some of the books are in short supply, we must reserve the right to substitute others of equal or greater value in The Trinity Library. This special offer expires October 31, 2006.

Order Form

NAME ____

ADDRESS _______________________________________

____

TELEPHONE ____________________________________

E-MAIL ____

Please:

❑ add my name to the mailing list for *The Trinity Review.* I understand that there is no charge for single copies of *The Review* sent to a U. S. address.

❑ accept my tax deductible contribution of $ ________ .

❑ send me ____ copies of *Not Reformed at All.* I enclose as payment U.S. $ _________.

❑ send me the Trinity Library of 60 books. I enclose U.S. $500 as full payment.

❑ send me the following books. I enclose full payment in the amount of U.S. $ _________ for them.

____

____

____

____

The Trinity Foundation
Post Office Box 68
Unicoi, Tennessee 37692
Website: http://www.trinityfoundation.org/
United States of America

Shipping: Please add $6.00 for the first book, and 50 cents for each additional book. For foreign orders, please add $1.00 for each additional book.